THE LIONESS OF JUDAH CHRONICLE 31

A Metaphor of Strength, Misjudgment, & Truth

Panagiota Makaronis

KREA PREA

ISBN: 978-1-7644581-3-9

Cover design by: B3STOW (TM). AI
Editor; KREA PREA (TM). Est. 2012
Written; Australia Victoria Melbourne Craigieburn

I dedicate this book to those who like to Hook you in line you up serve you a final & attempt to continue to feed off you from within!

"METAPHORICALLY SPEAKING"

AMEN

I am Asking for Recission
An Exemption to that Redemption, to the Rule

No explanation needed because apparently it seen as an excuse, by those who assume they can redeem scheme and follow up with an ending that was pending. Hunting you down & pretending they are your Friend. But behind your back they are scheming to harm you with…

The End of AMEN & the beginning of the OMEN.

PANAGIOTA MAKARONIS

INTRODUCTION

Chronicle 31 The Lioness of Judah A Metaphor of Strength, Misjudgment, and Truth. My Philosophy "This is my metaphor the language of a burden, not reality."; it is my way of dealing with the pressure of what Civilization has to offer. My way, of letting Humanity know; what I perceive is what I believe.

"If I don't see it, I can't believe it, if I don't manage the stress then I won't be able to claim my truth."

This is probably why many procrastinate, and others have unwanted addictions. You are misunderstood, let down by the system, because those who see you misjudge you and interpret you by mirroring you through their own self-worth. It tends to leave you suffering as you are struggling.

Instead of being given the benefit of the doubt, your energy is tagged. You become aroused by the trap, a trace left behind. It leaves you hitting a hold up, a test that has you forced to look within trying your hardest to fight of that demon that chose to enter your realm and hand you a mirage.

For those who misjudge create a war in your peace. Just to catch up and prove that they know you better than you know yourself. Wishing you hell so they can continue to raid in your head and get ahead and leave you for dead, starving for answers suffering in silence from the past not the present.

Who's to blame? Who's the reason you hit treason. Trapped in the middle of a bad season. Where your world is tarnished your dreams are varnished. Your dramas unfold and you hit a hold up waiting for the corrupt to return for another turn up. Where time does not stand still, life has no meaning.

Those who knew, had vanished, moved on and others have taken over their role. Accomplishing a goal a given reason to challenge you with a failed lie. A chance to release that beast that forced me to revive a follow up on a dive. Every time I hit a hold up, I found myself in the middle of a final truth.

I had to prove to whomever I was innocent, but the method was created by peace. When you are surrounded by Corruption the only thing that can serve you well from within was the energy that created chastity. The method was to praise me raise awareness serve me.

But all it did was harm me, it had me fail fall and feed off the trace once and for all. Little did I know I had competitors who were fighting for the same key, in the end I gave in for competing with them was no win. I made my mark created my piece mastered my craft where I shared with the world.

Sharing it with the world was meant to bring forth World Peace. But those who were competing for the same key decided the best thing was to harm me and find a replacement simultaneously. Someone who apparently is more worthy. Served a dishonourable race that trapped me.

It left me unbalanced, out of place, it created a piece. I was taken in and fed off with no limitations from within. I was torn left once again, raiding my head trying to come to terms with the fact the corrupt is a lead cut and a challenge to harm those who want to create an outcome to succumb.

There are no answers to that relay that had me press replay. Taught a lesson, picked up where I left off. Where the energy that created the piece returned and hit me with a feast. Unless you learn to manage stress, the journey can hit a holdup. Face a drama, that will harm you like no other.

You cannot process nor progress, without wondering. Because what you see is what you perceive. There is no lie to get by, nor a limit to the corrupts final, mission. For the path you choose is not the path that is chosen, for you; it is survival to the fittest. Once you lose your health you lose yourself.

The only way to overcome that outcome is create a balance that will serve you well. Before you stray and go the wrong way, stay true to yourself and try your luck and press replay. You must return the favour by forcing yourself to rewind, claim your game. Get back on track remain vigilant not violent.

There is no chance in hell to return repeat or unlock another flock. For the energy that sent you an electrical current to your current circumstance stated the wrong fact. It caused an effect and pushed you off track. Presenting you with a key to help you see; the energy that stated it also created it.

Alongside a challenge that paused an effect. Handing me an indication, a silence to a journey with no limitation. Serving me the truth and handing me the reminder, there was no presentation to that investigation. It was all part of a true lie, that took its time fed off the crime handing me an enigma.

Creating stigmata, because it took its toll and fed off the wrong. Handing you the edge of reason a curse that served you the wisdom to look before you leap. Take the energy that served you that synergy and prepare you for a road that has you release that beast; that forced you off the edge.

Until you see the truth unveil you become the perpetrator, creating war to bring forth peace where all along, you're the victim trying to remain strong. he who warned me there is no face to that trace just a heavy burden to erase. Before too long it was left to chance, now; blame is the game.

Overall Corruption within Humanity is a mess. Aggravated by the conquest, exaggerating beyond repair. The structure is based on a lesson that needs to be judged on both ends. You can't have one blame and leave the other wasting that train of thought because he is defeated; he has no feat.

In true fact cheaters always win at the beginning. In the end you catch them scheming for another inning. At what price, it depends if its corruption working at its best there is no faith or prop it is just another test to that conquest. After a while they get caught up in sneaking up on their victim.

Trying to create a brand-new system by feeding off their vision. I am a number one victim to that one. I had a dream shared it with the world those who were stalking me under the raider, saw me succeeding took a cheap shot and left me silently suffering. I gave in hoping, I for once win.

If only they knew, what dream, because all dreams become nightmares in-between. So, I went back for a vendetta and found myself in a position worse than the mission. On the hope I catch the perpetrator. Just to prove I am innocent all it did was make me look worse! What a bloody curse.

There are no winners or losers in this world only victims. We are all victims in society; the winners table can be turned to the losers. There is no stability to that table, it can rotate and reverse leaving some unworthy and others serving. Trying to feed off a dream that is less deserving.

Assuming that's how they will get in but winners never cheat and cheaters eventually never win. They observe serve and not feed off those who win. Because they know how hard those winners struggled to get in. They followed a rule took another route took the initiative and got out.

Overall, in Metaphor, "The Corrupt will always lie, cheat, trace, trap, trick and twist your words around. Cuff you up on the hope you swallow a razor blade, spit and cough out Blood." Amen

CHAPTER 1

◆ ◆ ◆

Who Was Empowered, & In Demand

It gave me a chance to create a trace at the end of the race. I will continue on my path as written by my free will. While I divide conquer and even out the end of that trend. The one that served me wonders and handed me a chance to face that trace at the end of the race.

I was to give in and hand the corrupt another chance to win. Feeding off the trend that faced me in the end. I had to face another predicament, clear the air and follow up on another faith. The one that took me in and presented me with a brand-new trend; a challenge that will save me in the end.

Where I get in and face my fear and reap my reward, all by the tearing the corrupts method in half. I was taught a lesson left to repeat had my test and repeated that piece. I was given a challenge that will serve me well. It brings me forward putting the corrupt through hell; having them face the truth.

Where this time around they lose hope and the trace to serve me well. It presented me with a case that forced me to erase it handed me a challenge that took me on a path that forced me to return a second chance to face a predicament. Meanwhile overcome an outcome a stigma to that enigma.

It had me face a trace, a given trend to release that beast. Fast-forward until the next, a given reason, just to hit back with treason. I decided to enter that realm and try my best to face me at my worst. So, when the pinnacle hit, it will hand them a trace that will serve me well at the end of the race.

For the truth set me free it brought me back to reality. Where the only thing that will serve me well will bring me forth. It will give me a challenge that will hand me a key, it will shock the system and hand them a trace, that will save me at the end of the race.

For I was given a challenge from within, trapped in the middle of a scheme to redeem. Then follow up on a trend that took me in and had me face another trauma from within. It was part of a trace that had me face a damaged thought. It had me end that drama dropping it all and facing another fall.

I hit a dead end that ended in a death threat. In the end it was heaving at me at every final bend; attached to my etheric cord. It had me walk into a challenge that had me face another waste. Then when the time come over-come another outcome. I was to get in witness it all and make my decision.

Try my luck, walk away from that hard ship that sent me packing. Handed me a chance to hit back in advance and hand it back to the sender threefold. For the old set me free, the new saw me easy by the time I reached my pinnacle the only thing that served me well from within was the task at hand.

It served me wrong, challenged me in ways that had me remorseful. I had to remain vigilant to the game, that taught me a valuable lesson. For yet again I was let down, put in a position to hand the corrupt a chance for a competition. Pushing me off the edge, in the corner, because I was in danger.

I was debating on when and how to claim the game. I had to remain in service, finalising the end, where I get in finalising that trap that had me face another creep at the end. For that trend that had me rally up the scores started again. I was stalling to find solace in the middle of my domain.

It had me reviving a new game, trapped in the middle, trying my luck to remain stable. Where every trace was uncanny, handing me a gamble. For the whole curse was to reverse, holding on to the past. An everlasting trace, that had me stepping into a path. It forced me to repeat a given reason to delete.

I was to hit back and faced with another treason. It was handing me an ending, that did not last a minute. The flame was a game that had never risen it was part of a conspiracy to push me off the edge, so I never reach my pinnacle and pledge. Not a second went by, where it turned out to be a lie.

It served me a decade of misinterpretation. A whole lot of dirty tricks and looks to match. It made no sense to my reality, it was off putting, each step had a wrong-doing. I was left to justify the action rely on whom ever to release the beast. Brought back to reality, a huge abre-action to that manifestation.

Those who were unknown, gave me a trace to end the road with a savage attempt to hit back and finalise that trace that was pending. It was based on a condition that led me toward a proposition that forced me off the edge. Ready to fight back and break the system, that had me facing another breach.

It gave me a second chance to reveal, revive and follow up on anther dive. It served me a clue; it forced me off the edge ready to review. It had me sense I was onto something huge; it had nothing to do to where I was heading. It was part of an ordeal that took me on a journey that was unsettling.

It was as if I was living a double life. The path I was on had me facing another warning. It drew a line in between the truth and the lie. I just needed to be patient repent and face a thread, where every trouble had me look ahead. Not regret a thing, because every endeavour had me face a vendetta.

Because it was all part of a debt that ended up a threat, it had me face another case. I was finalising that endeavour that forced me off the edge, straight into a trace that had me hit a dead end. It was forcing me to revive and follow up on a dive. Enough time for me to envision the truth.

It caused an effect and created a journey that will save me. All while the rest look within attempting to restore a challenge where they lose everything. For the journey was no longer pending. It was to fade and every trace will take the initiative where the trend will break the system.

For every challenge will turn against them. Feeding off the vision, returning the favour that had me face another competition. It was part of a phase that had me face another trace. I was left to hit back with a challenge, that will serve the corrupt a condemnation; save me, no trace nor trap to replace.

It will help me come first, return to repeat, rely on whom ever to press delete. For the curse come first the injustice had followed and during the whole ordeal, I was served well. It forced me to stay true, tune with my psyche. I was not going to lose sight, or a night of sleep just to put the corrupt at peace.

A chance to release, had me repeat and find peace. It was

part of an ongoing affair; it forced me to stay true. Continue on my journey like I never knew. It had feed off the old while I catch up and face another enigma, at the end of the race. Even though, the thought was creative the rumour was worse.

They were creating a terrible lie, that forced me to fight back. I had to face another trace at the end of the race. It served me well, brought me back to reality somehow. A trace that had me face a trend in the end, was astounding. A forthcoming event had me embracing a new clue.

It forced the corrupt to skip that too, then hit back and repeat a new improved journey. From the beginning, was embraced with a cause and effect. It had me come forth and repeat that trace with a debt in the end for that presentation. It had me obligated to hit back with a revelation, exempted.

I had no trace I was on the leaver, waiting to be replaced with another receiver. A treatment that landed me a role, was handled with care, it freed me from another scare. I had to overcome and repeat a new key; just to find peace and serenity. What I knew, who was to participate, had me speechless.

It was a given a part of the forbidden. It served me a chance to hit back for no reason. For it had me remain strong, it was part of an extension to release that beast. The energy that created that redemption. It was somewhat disloyal, it handed me false hope; a chance to evoke,

It had me return for one more season. A serious reason,

to step into the unknown and follow up on a tradition. A challenge that served me well and forced me to repeat caused an effect and pressed, delete delay and face another trace at the end of the day. While I put the corrupt through hell.

No ending insight, just a warning that will stop me from revealing another yearning. That skill that took me on a journey lined me up. It had heaved entering the unknown. It was neither heaven nor hell, it was an internal inequity, where the corrupt took it in and used it as an advantage.

They peaking Feeding off the injustice, challenging me as they repeat forcing me to hit back and delay another investigation along the way. The concept was surreal; the journey had a passive aggressive approach towards a dead-end destination. While remain sturdy and inline, towards a stalled task.

I was handed a presentation, that gave me a chance to repeat another investigation. Until the end a pressure that served the corrupt a challenge they cannot pretend. It was relying on whomever to repeat another endeavour. Served a second trail a challenge that will protect me from that trial.

I had to restore my energy once more. A faith that had me step into the unknown, creating an extreme offence. It warned me there was no task to join. Only a face to that trace, that had me finalise the end. Creating a backlash of information a desirable effect that will turn the corrupt against one another.

A debt that will return and face the corrupt in the end of that trend. For the edge had me trapped I was in the middle of a pledge. I was left to return, repeat step into a journey that forced me to press delete. Denying them access as I continue to release that everlasting beast.

What a frail return, that handed me the incredible in justice. It was forcing the corrupt to reveal revive and follow up on another trap a tension to get me back on track. they were given a chance to divide and conquer. Stalled, long enough for me to return and hand the corrupt the rough end of that trend.

I left it all to chance, I had no choice, that was the only way I could move forward and advance. I was put in a position where the corrupt were to follow up and try their luck. It was purely to override and feed off the trace that had me face another treasure. It was restoring what I thought was unravelling.

It led me to release that beast, a challenge that had me face another warning at the end of that theme that forced me to break that drama in-between. For what I thought was the end of that trend ended up becoming a challenge. It had me face an ending that was pending, and the corrupt surrender.

I was on the edge reformed ready to return for an informative event. Just so I can catch up and rise above and beyond what I thought was the last resort. All while they deliver and present me with a key. It will give me the opportunity to hit back with scrutiny. A challenge that will serve me well.

They were stirring trouble, waiting for me to fail; so, they can prevail. I had to remain stale from that feast that had me face another informal case. It had me yearning to clear the air and return the favour. Warning me, the only thing that come my way was the troubles that had me face another bad day.

All while I catch up and feed off the concept. It had me face another case, partly because the journey was too hard to replace. For the game that forced me to remain the same, had me return the favour. For the interpretation to that manifestation created a piece, it had me foreclose another voyage.

A faith to a case had me on the brink of facing a new endeavour. About to hit the corrupt with a vendetta. It had me separating what I thought was the last resort. In the fact it was the beginning of an everlasting task. A trend that stirred the pot, served right, to give the corrupt a chance for a fight.

After all, I reached my peak, hit a home run refining each pinnacle. An outcome that had me step into a trial and error. Just to find myself hitting a trace that forced me off the edge. It was restoring my energy and breaking the cycle that hit me with denial. For the definition to the mission was too high.

I had to convey, then convince myself otherwise, just to stay afloat. All because I hit a wrong note. The pitch was not as strong as anticipated, and the only way to impress was to claim another test. It was part of a twist to have me witness a lie, just to hand me a faith; less likely to get by.

It was part of a past endeavour, where I get in and gradually accept defeat. It had me forced to recreate a brand-new vision to that mission. I was to break the silence, fade that trade that caused the effects. warned of the first thing that brought me forward and the last thing that had me face a new inning.

When I hit the end of that graduation, it had me poisoned I had to clear the system and start fresh. Time took its toll and the healing process took effect; just to finalise that ending that was pending. It became part of a manifestation that led me astray; all while I press replay.

As if I had nothing better to do than feed off entrance to a failed entity. A given momentum that served me well at every retaliation. I had to set a precedent just to claim my thoughts. I had to lay low press replay and believe that the drama was too hard to relieve.

I found myself in the middle of a true rude awakening facing what I thought was already revealed. In fact, it was part of a test that had me process another conquest, to that measure. It forced me to revive a challenge. I had to remain positive for every test had me progress, continuing on my quest.

CHAPTER 2

◆ ◆ ◆

When The Corrupt Attempt To Follow It Through

I was on the mend, lining up for another dead end. Trying my best to pretend, nothing happened. I had no choice but to brew and renew, for what I thought was the last resort was over the top. It was the beginning of a new inning and the end of a trap, that had me pushed off the edge, back on track.

If I gave in, when the pot was hot, my journey will reach its pinnacle I would be stuck in a rut trying to redo and reclaim another clue. It had the corrupt serve me well, handing me hell. I was given a reason to hit back with treason, where the challenge was uncanny and my spirit unravelled.

I hit a trace to a case that had me forced to give in. It had me feed off the trauma that served me well when I hit the end. It forced me off the edge straight into the extreme. Warning me I hit an eerie momentum a challenge that will break the system. A trace served me a distance handing me a clue.

It gave me a second chance to brew over the new. The trace that will hand me an ending that will be pending giving me the impression I hit the Antichrist. An entrance to the unknown a key that will serve me it will gestation to hit back with a revelation. It was part of a case that served me an entrance.

It gave me the permission to hit back and break the corrupts improvision. Handing them the lack to fight back, no power nor a key to justify their action. Just a challenge to break the system and face another final degree. I was nowhere near the lead. I was working towards the end trapped in the old.

Trying to come to terms with a pathway that had me feeding off the old, confused me profusely. It was handing the corrupt a chance to confront me with a confession. It will break the energy that had me face another threat. All because a new breed created a new trend handing me power.

I had to regain conscious awareness again. Trapped in the middle of a curse, I could not rehearse. The test was part of a free ride to the other side. Giving me the impression the deception was nothing but part of a trend that had me face a dead end. It caused an effect and left me to release the beast.

It will make things worse, a chance for the corrupt to get in and win another inning. Trapping myself in the middle of a curse had me rehearse. I was let on led to believe the trace, was part of a case that had me reaching my pinnacle uncovering truth and releasing that demon that forced me off the edge.

I fell straight into a ditch pitched in and watched the corrupt face another inning. A challenge that will break the system and face what I thought was a reality kick. In fact, it was the beginning of a new improved venture, that served me well. It brought me back to reality all while I went through hell.

I was led on, left to repeat all while the rest remained strong. The challenge took me on a path that had me restore my energy once more. I was given a fight left to return for another hit, so when I caught up, I could undo that review and face the corrupt with one more point of view.

I was taught a lesson, left to hit the corrupt with a confession. All so I can come first and feed off the drama that had me face another revelation. It was a feast, at the end of that lease. It cased closed, just before I had a chance to invade evolve and finalise a story untold.

It had me face a challenge one that was about to unravel the theme. A scheme that had me questioning the corrupts method in-between. Forcing the corrupt to open up then own up, for the challenge was nothing but corrupt. It was a pathway served well; it had me foreclose a chosen spell.

Giving me the opportunity to delve into what I thought was the last resort. I was given a reason to cheapen the deal; it left me on the edge, sacrificing that trace that had me face another case. For what I thought and what it was worth, I had no recognition to that mission it was proposal.

It forced me to hit back with admiration, just to catch base. I was to catch up and feed off the corrupt leaving them suffering all while I get back and break that trap that had me warned I was nowhere near the end of my tither. I had to face my fear, break the trend and hit a dead end.

A challenge that had no freedom in the end, broke the system and led me towards a journey that gave me a reason to fight the corrupt back. All because the presentation was nowhere near the validation. It was part of a given momentum, that had me forced to hit back with redemption.

For what I thought was part of a given, had in fact left me facing another failed attempt. I had to bring forth a challenge that had the corrupt face me with a final release. It was chaos, poisoning my spirit at every formative trend a challenge that served me well in the end.

In fact, it had me face a warning, a case that served me well. A willingness to hit back at the end of that trend. For I was presented with a curse that took me in and fed off me from within. A failed impact, where I had to withdraw then take the trace and trap those who ignore.

Leading the pact, towards a journey to help me get back on track. A vision that had me face a failed attempt, had no repetition. The drama was unveiling; I was unravelling the last thing that had me facing another inning. Where the only thing that warned, me was left to the imagination.

I had to face a trace that was hunting me down. It was the last thing that had me forced to hit back with remorse. I had to release that one thing that had wailed me down. A past endeavour that served me well. I had to repeat a trend at the end. Creating a warning and then starting again.

I on the trace, ready to break the corrupt and face my truth. A challenge that had me forced to become recluse. For everyone I met had a plan and neither of those plans were going to bring me forth. For what I thought was part of the last resort, had me warned; there was no treasure or trace to replace.

It was as if I was given a reason to release that demon. So, when I reached my pinnacle, I could redo and reclaim another review. For the thorough response that kept me humble, had me heaving at every thorn. Where I caused an effect and broke the chain, entering another domain to the game.

An entrance, I could not replace had me stay alert. That is when I knew I hit the last and final review. Because every presentation had me serving the wrong deed. My past crept up on me and warned me I hit a final. I was ready and willing to face the corrupt and break the cycle.

I hit a final and in the end the trace had become part of a dead end. It was the last resort, and the only way I could press replay was in fact trace that case keep up with the program and follow through with another review. I had to lead by example, practice what I preach without, entering the wrong avenue.

While exiting and indicating what I knew, I had to face another review. Then lead the corrupt to a destination, where the common ground has no manifestation. It had me following up on a review so I can catch up and face what I thought was the last resort. All because the trauma had no preach.

I had to delete delay and face another bad day, purely to inform the corrupt that to catch-up was not part of the test, it was part of the quest that will serve me well at the end of that spell. Where every poison served me well it gave me a second chance to break the spell.

For there was no freedom, to get in and face another win. For every foundation had me state another revelation to that recommendation. For there was a face to that trace that had me follow up on another case. It will remain strong and when I hit a warning from within. It will revive another inning.

I will gain the wisdom to claim the indifference and face what the last resort could embrace. While I catch up and follow up on another inning. I got through trapping the corrupt right in the middle of the rough. For what I knew had me return for one more key. It served me well and faced me.

All while I went through hell, releasing that one thing that forced me to win handing me the power to confront and follow up on another passion at the end of that presentation. I had to face a trace that had me force to hit back with remorse without having to reward those who used me to record.

I hit an incur, travelled from one end to the next, trapping those who faced me on a curse they can reverse. It was part of a trace, where the trend had me break the curse return hot back and rehearse before I reverse the curse. I had to watch them confess, all while I give in and prepare myself.

I was experienced here; it took me in and faced me from within. Warning the corrupt I had no freedom to begin. A was given reason to hit back with treason, it handed me a case to give the corrupt a chance to replace it all. For that reason, I was hit with a second chance to back down and replace the crown.

For the walls were to collapse, there was no faith, all there was had me return. It presented me with a challenge that faced me with a trace. So, when I hit the end, the only thing standing was the corruption that left it withstanding. Where I get in and follow up on another inning.

Spinning the wheel in the long term, will not bring fortune. Because the wind is an invisible force can spin in both directions. Where every challenge can be turned around every foundation in meantime, I had to remain patient for those who knew, were unravelling another clue.

I had to step into the unknown, repeat an old flame. Little did I know it was a little white lie that was part of a dream that was meant to depart when I hit that everlasting raid. Where drama will bring peace in-between. Just to replace the old the new and the upcoming review.

I was hit with treason, for no reason. The foundation dropped and it handed me a chance to embrace that case and claim another the mission at the end of the race. It caused an effect and forced me to reduce another revelation to the next final destination. A proposition that brought me forward.

I was watching it all come to an end, finalising that dead end. It had me collapsing, where the system failed and everything that had come, forward masking taped me. It forced me to repeat and repel against the outcome. After all, I was taken out of that hell hole about to repeat another spell.

It had me Spoiling the method, that brought me forward. I fell into a trap that had me face the facts. It turned against me and pushed me off track. It was based on repetition that served me an appraisal. No vision to reverse the competition, for it was based on a frail termination to that investigation.

There were no competitors that could meet me halfway.

Unless they belted me to the ground unfairly. They left me suffering on my own severely handing me the indication I hit that final revelation. Releasing that demon that took me in forced me to release that piece with ease from within.

An effortless approach served me a key finally, an indication; I was invited to early. Where the manifestation to that congregation had me safe and sound. I had not reached my summit on time and the journey I was on had declined. It had me face a step, forward towards the wrong direction.

The thought had nested in my head, where it landed me a final role. It served me well at the of that trend that pushed me through hell. It handed me a brand-new conviction, about to follow up on an addiction. So, when they met me at the end of that trend it will prepare me for a dead end.

For what I thought would be the last resort, had me face a trace, stepping into the unknown. It was helping me state a fact in the end. It caused an effect and had me pretend. It forced me to repeat and rebel against those who return and finalise that feast while I press delete.

Because I was not there yet and the corrupt knew. They decided to pick up where they left off and attempt to break me right through. Assuming the spirit I had was fragment of my imagination. In fact, it was my truth and the only way I could get through was invade in the corrupts final review.

Feeding off the concept so I can skip that too had me

return for one more review. For what I thought gave me a second chance to hit back in advance. Warned me of what was to come from that outcome. For every time I peeked, the drama will sail through I would have to pick up where I left of.

For the conclusion took me on a journey that served me well. It warned of what was to come from that outcome. All so they can skip escape and follow up on another step. Where I had to face a trace that stated a fact and gave me the opportunity to fight back with scrutiny.

A direction that led me to face another resurrection, had presented me with a key. It lined me up from a wrongdoing. I hit the end of that trend warning me I was unbreaking forcing me to release that beast. I was determined to make it happen, a destination it had me ruining the corrupts finally.

It had me emotionally unstable, leading me to a declaration that served me a warning from that scheme that had me redeem independence from that disloyal theme. For I needed to reserve the right to return and face another entrance to that trap that led me off track.

It was too hard to portray and the challenge that served me well all the way. I was hit with a challenge another bad day. An investigation, creating a piece that had me face another feast. I was forced to hit back with remorse than follow up on another case that had me repeat another chase.

Where I was given a reason to hit back with treason. Break the mission and feed off the competition. I had to face a new trend break the system and trace that case again. For that trend caused an effect and handed me the opportunity to return for another treason.

Where in the end the only thing standing was the last thing that had me face another inning. For the end of the race, had me forced to replace and face another case. Where I get in and pretend that the only thing I could reveal was the last thing that had me face another ordeal.

I was given a chance to hit back in advance, where every feast at the end of that piece had me on the edge waiting for the atmosphere to claim another division to the game. I had to face the end of that enigma that had me lose my whole lead at the end of that breed.

I was given a chance to hit back in advance. Where every challenge had me forced to hit back with remorse, creating a final that had me stand up and finalise that tradition that left me swimming in filth trying to claim a division. A damnation that had me cause an effect presenting me with a defect.

I had to take a gamble it had me face another scheme. A game for me to state a fact and feed off the dream in between, with no apparent reason. It had me replacing the old the new and the strategy that handed me energy. It threw me off track, took me on a path that was stalling.

The corrupt saw me as an easy target, they tried to reveal a lie; just to open up an investigation. Attempting to face me, with a thought that had me forced to hit back with remorse, became unsettling. I hit a faith that served me an interest, so when I created the piece, I could return.

I was to follow up on a feast, a new improved goal. It was part of another presentation to that reserved me the right to disclaim a new game. It was gambling that trace that had me reserved for another case. An imperative step into the next final destination, it became vile and I hit denial.

For that situation that led me astray, it was putting me through scrutiny, all the way. All while I went through the trace that forced me to give in and break the cycle from within. For that journey I was put on had me face another entity from within. My trace was final my key was holding me up.

I was in denial in the end, as a result it had me forced to rely on the corrupt to come forward. Or else I would be stuck pending for another never-ending challenge. A trace that served me well at the end of the race. All while I delete a trace, denying me the truth at the end of that trend.

It forced me to pretend give in and face another challenge from within. It had me hooked, forced to replace the old start new and feed off the review. I was torn in more than one direction. Hitting the corrupt at every revelation. I was stepping down towards a level of a rude awakening.

Just to get a glimpse of a truth, a challenge that hit me and gave me the finals. A feast that had forced me to release and find peace. It had me face the corrupt with denial, where every thought had me pretend that the trend was final. I was protected but still living in denial; practicing what I preach.

The only way out will have me living a lie, all so they can get by. It was part of a role that will feed off me and present me with a key that will have me trace another test. It had me forced to hit back with remorse. All while giving me the power to reduce and break the silence.

CHAPTER 3

◆ ◆ ◆

When The Corrupt Find Oppurtunity To Stir Me Up

What I assumed had me face another trace; it served me a sentence. It led me towards a journey that created the piece, it had me constantly on the run feeding off the outcome. I was to feed off the treason that put me in a position worse than I could imagine.

I was on the edge forced to pledge, feeding off the trace that had me face another case. For the trend became a dead end and I hit the end of that freeride with the imagination that brought me back to salvation. I was given an entrance to a place that served me well.

It gave me a second chance to put the corrupt through

hell. A trace that forced to accept defeat. It handed me a clue to hit back vengeance. It caused an effect and broke the silence, right through. It had me restore my energy once more. It was part of a curse that served me well it had me come first.

I was warned and the only thing that come my way was a challenge that made me press replay. I reached my point of no return; I took that toll and broke the trace, trying my hardest to replace. For I was given a challenge that will serve me a piece. It had me presented me with a key I could not release.

A final journey that will harm he who harmed me. Sacrificing that inner being that served me well. A trace that caused an effect and handed me the trend that broke the cycle in the end. It replaced me with the old the new and the final to claim that had divided and conquered all the same.

I was hit with a challenge that had me face another trace. It gave me a second chance to pretend that I had no reason to serve the corrupt a final treason. I went through trying to overcome that spell only to witness the journey was cleared and the trace was revered.

I had faith what I had was a trend to serve me well in the end. I was taught a lesson left to repeat restore my energy and press delete. It had me overcome what I thought was the last internal case. A challenge that had me trace another case. A second trial that served me denial.

It had come to my attention the trend come to fruition.

It hit me with superstition, served an invasion that caused an effect and broke the system. I was taught a lesson left to rise above and beyond. I had to face them when the time come where I end up hitting a home run.

Where I get in state a fact and feed off the entrance to get back on track. It had them all standby, clearing the way it had me waiting for a trace that served me well. In the end of the race my head in trying to state a fact all while I get back on track. Reaping a reward and finalising that tremor.

I was handed a dilemma, a review that served me well. It presented me with a given, all so I can catch up and feed off the treason, it handed me a dead end that took me in and put me in a position worse than I can imagine. The shock to the system handed me revision and brought me forward.

It had me face another given, I was taught a lesson and left it to chance, belting the corrupt in advance. It broke me enough to have me rise above, for the tension served me a final redemption. I was given a chance to prove that the energy that served me well, forced me to hit back and go through hell.

In the end of the mission there was a final competition. It forced me off the edge stronger than ever. It had me facing another dilemma. It was part of a curse that took me in and faced me from within. I had to face my fear, fast forward to the next, just to create a trace I could contest.

Warning me that the energy that had me face another

contest. It became obvious that I was left oblivious, it had me facing a return to a trend that forced me to hit a final anomaly. It was part of a challenge that was inconsiderably alarming. It was a dilemma that caused an effect and faced me.

Every thought handed me the last resort. It was part of a true rude awakening. A trace that had me face an extension to that redemption. It forced me to repeat a competition, restoring my energy and repeating the mission. What I thought was part of a creative trend, had me return and start again.

It had me face a dead end; it handed me a thought empowered by the truth. It had me hit back with the last resort. Where I was given a reason to return for one more season. I had cut the cord claim the game feed off the mission and rebuild from the old repeat the old with the new.

I then had to create a challenge, that will serve me well right through. I was hit with a tremor that had me protest. It warned me I hit a final a generic key, that served me well independently. For the one thing that had me face a new inning, gave me the power to delete delay and devour as I press replay.

For that trace was part of a given it had me face another competition. Held hostage to a final degree have me contest and the corrupt confess for that conspiracy was nothing but a contest. It all come to fruition, just to feed off the mission that handed me competition.

Stating a fact and hounding the corrupt had brought me

back to reality. It had me fast forward so I can get back on track. It was part of a rewarding challenge that took the corrupt in and handed me a key. It forced me off the edge ready to repeat and follow up on a pledge.

Just to catch up and face another trace, at the end of the race. Creating an emblem that will bring me forward. Every time I hit the end, for I took it all in broke the system faced another mission. Trapped the corrupt at every competition. A trace that served me well at the end of the race.

For what created the piece also had me face another feast. It served me well presenting me with hell and handing me the condition to break the corrupts second trial. It was hitting me intuition facing me with a competition. For I had to give in and face the corrupt with a challenge they cannot win.

I was forced off the edge, hardening my soul allowing my spirit to take over. Because I fell and lost control, I hit a trace that served me well. I hit a predicament that lined me up for a feast. I was taught a lesson and took it all in waiting for the corrupt for another chance to win.

A division to a game that had me remain solid drove me to a destination that served me well it served me the right to embrace a case that warned me I had no chance to embrace another trace waiting to claim what I thought was the last resort. It handed me an encore at the end of that restoration.

It had me switched on, hot to trot ready to return and heave at every momentum. Where every final review served me well, it took me and in faced me from within. It forced me to interrogate with intricate detail all while I investigate a trace from within. Giving me the opportunity to write a wrong.

It led me towards a journey that was covering up another rude awakening. For what I thought was the last resort gave me a second chance to return to break the trace and put the corrupt in a trance while I end the race with a transition to that mission that handed me an intension.

For I was given a chance to hit back with treason, challenging the corrupt for no reason. I was on the move trapped in the middle of a challenge, that had me restore what I thought was the last resort. It gave me a chance to hit back in advance reveal another key and have the corrupt desire.

Handing them no resurrection had me facing a destination, that was troubling the corrupt at every evaluation. It was leaving me in the lurch, waiting for the corrupt to come first. Where every thought took me on a mission a given, handing the corrupt a dead end at the end of that proposition.

I was left to try to hit back and face another impact. For every challenge stirred the pot it gave me a second chance to hit back in advance. For the trend that had me face a dead end. Also landed me in a role that stirred the pot and handed me an evaluation to return for one more key.

All while I hit the end of that trial, that poisoned me. It

positioned the corrupt to hit me with dignity. For every trick that left me wallowing in self-pity. A trace that restored my energy and gave me a truce. I was hit in between the old thew new and the final review. For I was given a release to that feast.

It forced me to fight back hit the end of that trend, a given a chance to delay it all. Create a deception that will lead them towards a journey that will break the trend. It had me feed off the traitor who served me well in the end. I was left to repeat a claim and deprive he who saw me as an easy target.

The one thing to help me come alive, served me well; it forced me through hell. For the corrupt challenged me and pushed me into an oblivion, it taught me a lesson and left me to repeat and compose a deception to that mission. It forced me to rebel against the corrupts tradition.

In the end the game was part of a gamble that took me further than anticipated. It was part of a trend, so I don't loose and fall into the same and go insane. I had to follow up to the next destination. Face the facts, trace a given and claim a new disposition. I was hit back with admiration.

In the end of that trend, I was led to believe that every challenge will help me conceive. Where in the end I felt lost trapped trying to get out of a dead end and a death threat in the end. For the race had me praise the corrupt and force my way in feeding off the concept so I can claim another win.

The energy that had me on the edge, had me facing that key. It had me warned I was nowhere near I was meant to be. I had to return to a presentation that took me on a pathway well deserved. A desire to conserve the old to remember the lie so when I enter the present I cut all ties.

The corrupt had me on the edge, when the challenge roughed me up. Giving in, was giving the corrupt a dead end to that everlasting curve. It had me restore a given a chance to hit back with recission. I had one more chance to line up and break the corrupt at every final admission.

I was given a presentation to repeat then manifest the next destination. Report the old, start new face a given and reap a reward, just to catch base and feed off the case. I had to lead the corrupt to a destination that forced me off track. Just to get into that righteous path the one that served me well.

It was part of a road that will hand me a clue. A given reason to break the cycle at every disposal, then create war in the corrupts revival. It caused an effect and broke the system, creating a trace that had me repeat another repetition. It was giving me the interpretation; I hit the end of that transition.

For I was on the move trapped in the middle of a trauma. It served me a brand-new honour in the horizon. It had given me a proposition that will hand me a revelation, just to relay a message to the corrupt final manifestation. Where there was no interrogation just a follow up to the next destination.

It had me forced to return and face another given, it took me on a journey that served me my rights and a chance to hit back with a challenge that stalled. Giving me the impression I hit the end of that deception that forced me to retaliate and hit the corrupt with an ending that was pending.

A challenge that was never ending, had me face a referendum. It forced me to repeat repel and stir up a bit of trouble so I can put the corrupt through hell. I was to feed off the tradition that stirred trouble. It had me return for a competition; in the end I could step forward and face another fear.

Because the corrupt stalled, it was keeping me hostage and them honest. That is when I knew I could stir the pot and create a challenge that will serve me well right through. I was left to repeat face another feat, so when I caught up at the end of that trend that handed me a challenge.

I was handed a second chance, that had come at its best. I must confess I had one to many challenges to overcome and the only way I could undo that clue was review and follow up on another point of view. I had to dive into a trend, that pushed me off the edge straight into a ditch.

I delved into a second chance handing me a trance. When I hit the ending that was pending, the free ride will overcome and hit me with a downside. I hit that dead end finally, on the mend. A trace that will create a rude awakening. A challenge that stirred the pot and handed me an evaluation.

I had to get in freely state a fact create a piece follow up on a trace. It was giving me the power to repent and the energy I needed to reclaim another division to a game that had been pending for quite a while. I was not awarded for my hard efforts, when the trend became part of a free ride.

Trapped in the middle of a condition that had me rise above that admiration. Warned me I hit the end of that trend that served me a willingness to start again. The concept changed the corrupt stopped and the journey fell into a hold up. I hit new review claiming what I thought was part of the last resort.

A proposition that served me well handing me the on-going profession to face the corrupt and feed off the mission. Because the corrupt had other ideals it re-warded me and took me on memorable journey. Where every destination had me face another condition to that mission.

The method was cunning, the leisure to that measure had me overpowered. I was pleasing the corrupt and forced to hit back with a final frontier. It was creating a piece that served me well it presented me with a chal-lenge that had me step into a path that faced me when I hit the end of my tither.

I was watching the corrupt warn me of what was to come from that outcome. I was forced to wither step-ping into the unknown with a trace that served me well at the end of the race. It had me face on the other end of that trend hitting that saga with a dead end.

I was hit with a syndicate; several were on my raider waiting for me to fail so I never prevail. It led me to believe a lie; it gave me a challenge to help me get by. All while I give in and feed off the trauma that served me well from within, I was finally on the mend creating a final trend.

It was my way of accepting the fact I was being torn in more than one direction. I was pleasing the corrupt at every deception, I had no idea there were several sitting on my resurrection. Wasting valuable energy trapping me at every manifestation.

For what I thought was part of the test was the last resort to the corrupts final feast. A given reason to harm the corrupt at every treason. It had me on the run developing a new gun. I was on the other end pretending while the rest had done nothing but hand the corrupt bad luck.

I was losing my cool creating a repetition at the end of the mission. A trace that will serve me well at the end of that race. It had me condition the mission and repeat after the fact for every challenge pushed me in the corner and broke me when I hit the end of that trend, pushing me back on track.

Serving me well had created a back lash of information; causing an effect. All while creating a challenge that had me debating what end will break that trend and what faith will help me start again. I was on the brink at the end of my tither where at the end of that manifestation I faced another tremor.

It brought me back to a given, all so I can hit back with a transition, to that mission. When I hit the energy of what was to come from that outcome. The trace had me face a given, sending me back to a final feast to clear the old start anew feed off the trap that had me forced to review.

A resurrection to push me in the corner and face me at every trend had me forced to redo and reclaim another review. I thought a trial and error had ended up harming me at every vendetta. It broke the system forcing that spirit to redo another bad day and the reason with me all the way.

I had to release that beast had me on the edge, returning the favour and reclaiming a new pledge. I was to release that demon that had me return for one more reason. For each challenge tore me to bits, a season finally gave me a chance to plant the seed I need to succeed.

I was on the edge releasing that demon that forced me pledge. It had me face a trace restoring my energy. Feeding of the trend that had me break the system in the end. I had to trace that case that led me to believe I was nowhere near that energy to harm me when I hit the end of that synergy.

While I reach my pinnacle I could indulge and face another trace at the end of that case. I had to repeat trick the corrupt at the end of that trend. It served me well and handed me a dead end in the end, forcing me to return and start again. Trapped in the middle of an appraisal that handed me survival.

When I hit the end of that transformation the only thing that served me well was the last thing that put me through hell. The thing that pushed me in the corner had me face another given. Where I realize the journey was not as dramatic as I assumed it was part of a challenge that had me consumed.

CHAPTER 4

◆ ◆ ◆

The Grass Is Greener On The Otherside

For he who returned had a huge track record, carrying a burden. I was left to replace report and feed off the energy that had me hit a high rise at the end of that trend. I was on the brink that served me well it broke the trace that pushed me in the corner and served me well.

I had to state a fact get back on track and feed off the concept. It had me repeat another trend at the end of that bruise that had me face Bad luck would follow me at every trough. Where I was given a chance to hit back in advance. It had me state a fact create an impact at the end of that trend.

It gave me a chance to get back on track following up on a piece. It trapped me in the middle of a feast. I had to release a challenge that served me well, it forced me to repeat and follow up on another spell. Just so I can get in and claim another win. For what I thought will break the system made me sin.

All while I give in and find peace, handing the corrupt a trace so I can complete my task. I had sweetened the deal faced another ordeal; serve that trend a dead end. I was trying my luck to repeat and hand the corrupt a chance to press delete. I had to face a given, just to hit back with treason.

Meanwhile follow up on a presentation, that had me face another conviction to that mission. I was on the path of creating a piece, all while I was debating what I had on show. For what it was worth and what was to come, it had me return and replace another outcome to that case.

For that trend served me well in the end. It was part of a journey that will clear the air and falsely make the corrupt step into my real m and face me with the intension of creating redemption. I was taken back hit with a trace that had me step into another trend in the end.

Every follow up had me foreclose a trend. Taught a lesson, creating a new trial in the end. I had to face a trace, pretend, feed off the dead end. I was on a mission to disclaim a follow up on a game. It had me gambling everything, to remain the same. I had to follow up on a clue and create a better avenue.

It had me raid the head of those who used me to get ahead. In the end of the trace there was a second trial, it had me on the edge of a given. It will serve me well where the energy had me face another spell. Surrendering what I saw in my peripheral vision had me witness another decision.

For what was to come from that outcome had me stepping into a lead that sailed through. It served me well had me come to be and everything that lad me to where I was meant to be had me face another true reality. Nowhere near the end for where I should have been had me start again.

I was tricked into an oblivion, trying to release the beast. My thought patterns changed the drama rearranged. It raided my head blowing everything out of control, I could not see the clear picture. Theat is when I knew I hit a new vision to that interruption that served me a new competition.

The corrupt were trying to belt me constantly, all so I never look beyond or look ahead. It gave me a chance, to restore my energy in advance. Releasing that demon that forced me to repeat, handing me the energy to convey, convince the corrupt there is no way out just a chance to erupt in advance.

A share of that trend had me face a dead end. It gave me a second chance to hit back in advance, trying my luck to pretend where every final handed me a creative stability to hit the corrupt with unity. For that trace was a dead end. It was the beginning of an entrance, a second trial with a vengeance.

It forced me to hit back with a united front. Where the influence that I had was being tarnished by the corrupt. For there was no trace to give in and no challenge to win. I had to feed off the case take another minute to accept that the loyalty in the end handed me disloyalty.

I had to heave at the end of the race. Then feed off the win so I can claim another voyage to the game. I was given a presentation that served me a wrong investigation. It caused an effect and handed me the result that served me a truce to that investigation.

The only thing that had me forced to hit back with remorse, was a challenge that gave me a trace. It forced me to peak and face another given. Just to give the corrupt a chance to confess handing them a dead end at the end of that trend. It led me towards the result that served me well.

I was on the brink of creating a new link. Where every challenge served me a case and presented me with an evaluation that brought me forward straight into the next destination. I was outsmarted by the corrupt left to release the beast. For I was on my own outnumbered and ganging up on.

It had me in the middle in the end of that spell trapped trying to get through. I was warned of what was to come from that outcome it gave me a second chance to hit back in advance. Where in the end the race had me face another case. A given case to hit back and replace.

A trace that served me well and handed me the internal investigation. It had me hit another manifestation to that trial that error and that cunning review that forced me to undo and claim a challenge to the game. For the one thing that forced me off the edge had me face another feast.

I was taught a lesson that had me face another test. It gave me a second chance to belt the corrupt in advance. For the end of that trend had me face another given, all while I was to repeat and repel at the end of that forthcoming spell. It was the last thing that had me face another trip down memory.

I was forced to come forth and feed off the tremor that had me reclaim another division to the game. For beating that handed me a trail faced me at the end of that tremor that forced me to hit back like no other. I was to delete that trail that served me denial. I had no reconnection to that deception.

All I had was a rude awakening. It led me straight into an enigma that restored my energy at ever stigma. I was to feed off the expense that took me in and faced me with a trap that had me forced to win. It had given me the impression the journey was loyal, and the trace was a given.

I had to do to take a glimpse of what was to come from that outcome. It gave me the impression the corrupt hit a revision to that manifestation. So, when I reach that final revue, the adventure I once knew had me survive and hand me a brand-new drive. Surrendering at every tribe.

Even the time where I to remain silent and keep alive. It had me reclaim another train of thought it gave me a chance to belt the corrupt in advance. Repeating the end of that trend that brought me forward and broke that system. It had me focused repeating a dead end in the end of that trend.

All so I can survive trap those who come alive. It had me feed off the trace that hit back at the end of the race, facing another caused an effect giving me the impression I hit a deception that landed me a role to the next manifestation. All because he who knew, and he could not wait to hit me in advance.

The trap forced me to overlap and create a challenge to get back on track. It had me in the middle of a trap that served me a trial an error and a final destination that will give me the power to overcome another embarrassing outcome. All while he surrenders and find my way through facing a review.

I was in the middle of a surreal ordeal, a trap to lead he who harmed me towards a destination that forced me to reclaim and feed off the ordeal that took me in and fed off me from within. For the corrupt had me face another key it caused an effect and handed me a credibility to get back on track.

I had to face a case line the corrupt up with a trace that served me a willing ness to hit back with diligence. For I was on the mark creating a curse where every trace served me well and caused an effect and put me through hell. Working towards a destination that will finalise every manifestation.

I had to condition the vision and follow up on a mission. It had me returning for a favour all while I hit back breaking the trend so I can start again. It had me facing a competition that warned me I had no force to hit back with remorse. What I had was a given, to present the corrupt with a warning.

A brand-new mission had come to fruition; I was trapped in the middle of a trace that had me forced to hit back with the same case. I was taught a lesson left to debate hit back and face another trace at the end of the race. I had to entrap and hand me a face that had me forced to hit back with a case.

All while I get back on track, and feed off the corrupt, it gave me a second chance to hit back in advance free myself from another challenge hit back while I create a trace to hit back and erase it was part of a faith that handed me a dead end at the end of the race.

I had no faith or the challenge to get back on track, what I had was a feed to give the corrupt another chance to get back on track and face another tactful event. I was given permission to hit back with a conviction that stalled long enough to face another trace and hit back at the end of the race.

I was given a reason to hit back with treason. I was off with the trend it had me face a dead end, overlap another given so when I reach that peak the rejuvenation will return and hit back. Facing me with an expense that served me well at the end of that forthcoming spell.

I was to give in; on the condition I can face a trace. All because I was given a total anomaly to that tradition that handed me a competition. I was left to restore my energy feed off the trend that had me on the go. ready to hit the corrupt with a dead end on the other end.

It was to give me a chance to hit back in advance. Trap those who condition the mission and follow up on another competition. I was to cave in on the concept challenge the corrupt then when the pot was hot creating a piece, that will force me to redo and reclaim a review.

It had me caving in on the concept all while I was hitting a home run. It had me face another trace serving me well and presenting me with a clear conscious. A challenge that had me face an affair it was pushing the corrupt in the corner hitting back with despair.

A challenge that come to be had me praising the corrupt so I can claim another game. Where they lose every cause an effect, it will force them off the edge, form a prioritization to that manifestation that served me a confirmation. I was hit and forced to reminisce, straight into a pledge.

Warning me, that every key; will give the corrupt catastrophe. I had no time to repent repeat nor even present he who took me in and tried his luck to feed off me from within. It had me face another deception to that resurrection. I had to press delete delay and follow up on another bad day.

I was torn at every finally creating a test. It was to help me light a match catch up and break the corrupt. For what I had was a trial an error and a simple task to sample the corrupts method. I was hit with a dangerous endeavour a given chance to erase that case and hound the corrupt at every trace.

It handed them a key that will fail them intuitively. I had to claim that vendetta no time for remorse. I was given a chance to hit back with a good cause. I was stepping into the unknown a challenge that had me sacrifice what I thought was suffice. The service had me turned and drama returned.

I took it all in and fed of that individual who assumed he can weasel his way in. For I was left to pretend took a moment to face another trace, so when I caught up, I could embrace a trend at the end of that dead end. For I was given a reason to face another treason chasing the corrupt at every season.

For every drama had me forced to hit back with a cause and effect. It led me to believe that every faith had me forced to hit back with remorse. Where I was given a challenge, to return for one more turn of events. It had me stepping into a breakthrough; warning me the time had come.

I hit a praise a powerful trace an outcome that had come to fruition. I had to break the corrupts system and leave them in a daze. With a faith less likely to achieve a drama worse for wear, for it served its purpose an error, that handed me a vendetta. I had to reclaim a follow up on a game.

It had me face a treason to enter a new season. I was hit with a vendetta towards an endeavour. Putting the corrupt through hell all so I can claim a point of view. A second trial to harm the corrupt at every vile. For every season changed and every reason gave me a force to hit back with remorse.

So, when I reached the trace, the given reason was entrapment. I had to remain silent, enforce the corrupt to repeat and follow up on a heave. A challenge that will serve me well and feed off the concept and put the corrupt through hell. A trace that had me face a new prospect.

I had to claim the game, give the corrupt a chance to remain the same. So, when I reached my pinnacle, I could undo that clue and create a brand-new review. It forced the corrupt to own up to every crafty event. It handed me unworthy debt; it had me work towards a journey that was humble.

A test that was hounding the corrupt at the end of that request; watching them confess. It was to hand me a key a reenactment to road that serve me contingence of information in a row that hit me ruination to the corrupts final destination. I hit a hold up a challenge that will serve me a round up.

It was enough for me to repeat repel and follow up on another given spell. Where every challenge had me forced to hit back with remorse, every trial took me on a journey that served me an anomaly. I had to repeat a trace that gave me a chance to service that trend. It hit me with a purpose and no final.

I was taken for granted, left to redeem then follow up on a theme that had me face a trend at the end of that forthcoming event. The skill was uplifting the drama faced with a scheme in between. I was taken for a ride, left to overcome a trend. Then when I least expect it, feed off the result in the end.

It had me face a case, trap that test and have the corrupt hit back and attempt to embrace what I thought was the last resort. I hit a preparation to the next destination where I hit an interrogation. I was facing a conflict of interest so I can pass another test and feast of that manifestation.

A journey that haunted me at every final destination. It presented me with a kind heart and wrongdoing. It had me on the edge, hitting back and protecting my soul, so I don't lose track. I was taught a lesson left to preach, started a fight creating an anomaly so I can get back on track and feast.

It presented the corrupt with another threat, just so I can catch up and press delete. Where I sat and who was on the other end had me facing a dead end. Where every thought had me courageously hit back and face another trace given a reason hitting back with treason.

A pointless affair that took me on a journey that left me totally in despair. I was given a chance to return the favour in advance. All so I can get back on track and present the corrupt with a final impact when I reach my pinnacle I could undo and feed off the trauma that got me through.

In the end of that debt, I was given a reason to follow up to the next destination. Just so I can catch up and break that cycle that had me face another testimonial. In the end I was stuck trying to provoke and prevent the corrupt from starting fresh serving the corrupt a sentence so I can protest.

It had me on trial, waiting for the corrupt to hit me with denial. I was ready and willing to stand my ground and feed off the trace, that stood the test of time. It had me face another united front; it had me cover up a condition that had me feast of that beast that served me well.

It had me hit from the ground up, forced to hit back with remorse. I was put in a position left to present the corrupt with a brand-new quest. It forced to repeat return and praise those who assumed the world handed them Glory. In fact, it served them well and put them through hell.

I hit a feast and had forced me to hit back with remorse. I was on the mark creating a task, forced to prevent the corrupt from returning for a yearning getting back on track. I was on the quest returning for one more yearning, heaving at every thought following up on the last resort.

I was the mask hitting back with a task waiting for the right moment to repeat and rebel against that upcoming spell. I was hit with a request that served me well and presented me with an upcoming spell. Then when the time come hand the corrupt a dead end in the end of that outcome.

In the end I was left to hit back with a dead end, a trace that had me face another case. It had me on the edge waiting for the corrupt to return and feed off the trace that had me face another case. It was warning me the only thing that come to be, was the last thing that hit me from within.

CHAPTER 5

◆ ◆ ◆

Time Flies When The Corrupt Lie

It had me facing another test, where I had to give in. Because I was stabbed in the back by those who were trying their luck to hit me run and hand me Bad Luck. I had to find a way to accept that deception, create a brand-new manifestation. I was left to catch up, project and hand the corrupt a death threat.

The reality to that deception had me face a competition. In the end it was all part of a trace that had me dramatizing the end of the race. Instead of accepting the fault it had me rising above and beyond creating a challenge that had me return to hit back and face me with bad luck.

I was taught a lesson, trapped in the middle of a trend, that had me face a dead end. I could not come terms with the fact my life was a lie. I was mortified the shame of that whole scenario ruined my chances of creating a piece. It had me face another tradition to that mission that served me release.

I was living in filth trapped in guilt projecting it and holding onto a grudge while the corrupt face me with potluck. all while they were on a mission hitting back with revision. It had me restoring my energy and claiming a request from that contest. where I had to repeat and face another trace.

Where in the end I was given the freedom to pretend. It created a pitch that served me well. Forced to go through hell, so when I caught up, I could return the favour and face another tradition to that proposition. It had me return repeat all while I catch up and press delete denying the corrupt access.

It had turned the mission into a frail failed attempt. It served me a presentation, that was handing me the evaluation to break that cycle. In the end of the race the given reason was replaced. That is when I knew I was handed a brand-new review a troubled mind to sweeten the deal.

It had me kindly catch up and face the corrupt. For every thought became part of a past restoration to that manifestation. Nothing could prepare me for the last resort. It had me chase a dream scheme in between. For the key that had me forced to repeat, had presented me with a brand-new anomaly.

For that trace had me foreclose another case. The assumption had become part of a redemption to hand me a resurrection brought me a broad Horizon of failed attempts giving me the impression I hit the everlasting depression. Assuming I would give in and hand them a failed deception from within.

It became the way out, and the corrupt hit a holdup they were out of line. I had to follow up on a time where there would be a barrier between the kind heart and the severity to that case that had me face another conscious awareness giving me the power to undo and devour, all while I divide and conquer.

The trace became harsh It hit the end of that task. Reaching my summit, had me preaching what I knew all so I can get through. For the challenge had me refine and create a new trace at the end of the race. A challenge that had me waste another decade, trying to prevent an interference.

I was left to pretend and claim a dead end, all while I witnessed a faith less likely for me to eradicate. I took a chance to hit the corrupt in advance, faced another royalty to loyalty card that handed me a tradition to that composition, that forced me off the edge straight into a prediction.

Where I had become addicted to the mission and the trace had me face another tuition. I had to claim the game as a true rude awakening, a given response to hit the corrupt with a theme. So, when I reach my mission, the only thing that served me well, had me face another warning.

Interrogating the trace that had me forced to hit back and face another trend at the end of that dead end. For the corrupt will lose their intuition, it will hand me a competition. For the trace was part of a case that earned me a key. I was warned of the discrepancy, that had me face a trend in the end.

It had me restore my energy and start again. Handing me the power to repeat and devour. All while I divide and conquer, creating a warning will serve me a waning. Even though the trace was based on a given the end result had hit me with the forbidden handing me the energy to retaliate.

I had to restore my energy then claim another division to the game. It served me well at the end of that mission. Warning me the only thing that forced me to win was trace that hurdled when I hit thew end of that trend a tradition that served me calamity to the corrupts serenity.

A case that conditioned the mission so I can claim another competition. It forced me to review cause an effect and screw the corrupt right through. For what it was worth, the thought was balanced with a vision. It created the piece that had me face another tradition at the end of the mission.

Praising what I thought was a key to that dream that served me well in-between. I had wondered off left it to chance kindly stated a fact and created a piece that had me step into the unknown. I was taken for one reason left to embrace another treason. Warning me the earlier I rose the later I shined.

Even though I was taught early how to survive late, the challenge served me and had me facing a united front. I was forced to review feed off the clue a given a reason to decline their point of view. I had to disclaim another season; it had me face that trace that put me through.

There was no response, it had me forced to hit back with remorse. It handed me a manifestation to that presentation. That caused an effect and presented me with a follow up to the next catchup. It was part of a turn for the better, a trace that served me a tremor.

A second chance to belt the corrupt in advance. It was wrong how they turned it all against my free will, put me on a pathway that served me a skill. In fact, it had me stepping into a burn, that created a path; that had me face a wrath. I hit a dead end and created a trend.

It forced me off the edge straight into a ditch. So, when I reached my peak the energy that served me well presented me with an upcoming spell. For what I thought and what will come from that return, had me face a given. Repair repeat and follow up on another vision.

So, when I faced that trend I could start again, ready and willing to convey another bad day. Where in the end that feast that forced them to release had me on the edge trapped in the middle of a pledge. They were saving me, when I caught them in the act. Trapped them in between facing another demon.

The one that took me in, met me from within, tricked me into believing a lie. An assumption that took over the redemption. I was served a condition that forced me to repeat, handing me the revolution to an unresolved issue. I would have handed them the truce, if they handed me the truth.

In hindsight it all went sour, my soul wanted to devour so it can divide and conquer. For the corrupt were on a mission to repeat another competition. It had me face another trend where the corrupt went in lockdown hiding, creating a dead end to that threat; that had me forced to pay off a debt.

It had me on the edge trapped in the middle of a trial an error and final vendetta. A trace that caused an effect and created a trend that will serve me well in the end. It made me see that every key had me face another final review. Stalled long enough to feed off the trace that had me face a case.

They took me in and wanted to pretend that every point of view had served me an overcast. It was part of a release that brought out the beast, a creasing effect that had me step into another debt. It took me on journey that served me well. It forced me to review and face another scheme.

I had to redo and face another trend at the end. Waiting for the clue to override another review. It had me on the go presenting the corrupt with an outcome that will prevent them from hitting me and running again. I rescheduled that scheme that had me feed; just to redeem a theme in between.

It had me foreclose another event. It created a given, a leading response to a repetition, just to cause an effect and hit the corrupt with a competition. A mark that served its purpose, just to send the corrupt packing. For that mission had me on the edge, teaching me a lesson at every disclosure.

I was to give in and create an oblivion to the corrupts mission from within. Just to catch up and face another denial to that redial. It had me return for one more turn. An event that served its weight in gold. For I was given a trace, that served me well at the end of the race.

Warning me every time, I hit a theme the challenge stirred the pot. For the trend will calm the waters again and break the system. Hounding me to redo and re-claim another division, towards a game that served me well again. A true awakening from a past dilemma, it had forced to hit back with a tremor.

I had to follow up on a review, a past revelation. It handed me a clue and trapped the corrupts mission right in the middle of a competition. It had me sitting on their raider waiting for the right moment to give in and face another trace that was creating a tremor.

A constant reminder the journey was harder than I anticipated. For the energy that stalled was handing me the step forward to get out of that stagnant affair. It left me facing a trend that had me on the other end releasing that Demon that troubled me, again.

I had no time than the present to reclaim another division. For I was put in a position worse than I could imagine. The game became tender; the trial had become part of an error, where the entrance stirred the Ethar and handed the corrupt a dead end in the end of that terrible lie.

It had me about to fail return for another theme a drama that served me well in between. A trend that forced me to enter and start again. It had me face a case that forced me to reclaim another division to the game declining the corrupt method at every sanctum.

My sanctuary had been torn in more than one direction, where I hit a hold up with discretion. It forced me to release and vaguely try to find peace. While my world had collapsed and I had to pick up where I left off. It became the corrupts way of entering my realm, without my knowledge.

It had me exiting a trace that served me well at the end of the race. Where every pace took me on a journey, every step of the way. I was given a challenge left to the imagination. I hit a final road to recovery where every trend will give me the power to compel and comprehend.

Handing me the evaluation, to disclaim another validation with discretion. Presenting me with what I thought was the last resort. It served me a willingness to embrace another trace, at the end of the race. Before I fell into a second trial; a challenge that had me in denial.

I had to get in and acclaim that trend that took me in and created a journey that served me well from within. I had to case close that tradition to face another trend at the end of that mission. It was part of a game that served me the willingness to remain the same.

A challenge that took me in and faced me from within. It had me create a final frontier chasing an ending that had me forced to hit back with remorse. Rather than sitting in the back burner waiting for the challenge to arise, where the journey created a piece and served me well at the end of that lease.

I could not imagine anything worse than having to opt out after the fact. It had me face another trace that had me put me in position worse than I could imagine. I had put up with another curse to that verse. Because it was all part of a dramatic effect that took me in and broke the system from within.

For it had come to my attention that the corrupt hit me with redemption. A trend that served me well in the end. It forced me to repeat and repel, all while I pollute the corrupts method. For the purpose was served and the claim had me reach my potential and remain sane; all while I start again.

A proposition that had me face another vision to that mission, became part of an appraisal that served me a survival technique that had me face another case. It was part of a cleanse catch up and face another trace at the end of the race. They went for the killing spree; for no reason at all.

Handing me a proposition that made no sense to me at the end mission. It handed me on review to claim another scheme in-between. A trickery to that treason where they made a mockery of the whole situation. The scenario went sour; I had to return and devour and take every momentum with a stride.

I had to hit the corrupt with deception, handing them a reality check every time I was presented with a key. A tremor that served me a dilemma, it had me face another trace. There was no truth in the matter, and I was stuck trying to get out of that dilemma. It had me covering up the lie with the truth.

Just so I never catch them in the act, where every trace had me face another case. Creating an annulment to a disguise at that vice that had me waiting for that deception to claim another redemption. It handed me the redemption serving me the silence at the end of that treason.

A challenge that had me face a case, lined me up for another trace. A trend that had me hit a dead end, needed to be attended to without delay. There was a presentation that had me foreclose another bad day. It was part of manifestation that caused an effect and handed me a challenge.

It had me return the favour, troubling the corrupt at every ambience. A given momentum that had me step forward, claimed it faith in the end of that trend that served me a presentation conditioning the atmosphere that tied me down. It had me facing an expense that served me well.

I was chasing the wrongdoing, repeating a failed meeting. An attempt to break the silence feed off the admiration had me face another manifestation. The journey was not as rewarding as I assumed. The one thing that had me on the brink was the last thing that took me in.

It had me facing another inning from within. It created a manifestation that pushed the corrupt off that animation. I was to enter the Dead zone and follow up on a final a red thread of redemption. It served me well and presented me with a conviction that handed me a final decision.

It was part of a key that caused an effect and broke the system. All while I took it all in and fed off the recission to that condition that served me well and handed me a mission where I get in and feed off the composition. I was on the mend waiting patiently to start again when I realized I hit a dead end.

For every trace served me a given, I was taught a lesson and hit with a proposition. Where every thread had me waiting for the drama to entertain me. I had to remain silent at every respite where the only way I could start fresh was create a challenge that had me face a dead end.

I hit a warning and the only way I could return and press replay was face another blow up. For the corrupt were given a chance to hit me in advance. Trapping whomever they saw fit to hit me for they assumed they were legit. I was to look back and feed off the tremor all while I face another dilemma.

It had me trace another drama at the end of that tremor. It forced me off the edge straight into a ditch It caused an effect and faced me with a defect; it took me on a journey that broke the silence. It prepared me for a final revival, where the denial was based on a conspiracy that served me a chance.

I was to hit back in advance. It handed me a clue, preparing me for a challenge that will help me get through. The case had me face a warning a trace where in the end of the race; handed a proposal. I was to return for another disposal. Where every thought handed me a conclusion to that diffusion.

I hit the end of that tradition that served me a brand-new composition. I on the other end, facing a presentation. It had me forced to hit back with remorse. It was giving me the power to undo and devour. Claiming a vision to that mission that forced me to hit back with a final admiration.

It had me turned waiting for the corrupt to break there fast. Only to witness every challenge handed me a service, on the edge. Trapped in the middle of that pledge. A case that forced me to reveal and revive another trace wasting that momentum no longer.

For I was on the move creating a deception from that redemption. It had me face another trace giving me the impression I was hit with a disposition. For those who condition the mission claim what I thought had me on the edge presenting me with a wrong proposition.

Not only I was stuck in a rut but the road I was on had me face another trace. It had me hitting a prediction that will hand me a final disposition. A challenge that will serve me well hand me a given to put me through hell. Where the curse took a turn for the worst challenging the corrupt at ever verse.

CHAPTER 6

◆ ◆ ◆

Those Sheepish Beginings

The humble moments that stirred the pot, forced me off the edge. Straight into a deliverance, waiting for the corrupt to hit back with a second trial. A final review before I fell into a trap, that turned my life upside down and turned my light dim and left me suffering from within.

It silenced me, forced me to repeat only to find time took over. Instead, off the cycle bringing me forward I was taken for ride hit with a dead end in the end. Where it forced me to hide. It had me hit back with an emotional blackmail. Reuniting to the corrupts final attachment, spraying venom.

It served me the energy, that stalled to the point where I needed to break the silence. It hit the corrupt and for one moment I rose above it. With that moment of despair, I was taken for granted on a ride to the other side. No emotional detachment just the freedom to break the system.

All while it took me on a personal endeavour to hand the corrupt a vendetta. I was given a momentum that will take me back where I was meant to be before was hit with a failure. For apparently, I was not good enough and what I was aiming for was not part of that encore.

Where the only thing that had me face another win, was a cheap shot. Left shocked to the system just to get back on track for everything I knew was nothing but a return from past review. I was handed a lie, left to divide and conquer and break the dream that hit that scheme in-between.

It handed the corrupt a challenge from within; trapping he who returned to harm me. It gave me a second chance to hit back in advance. I was left to feel shame, release a demon to remain the same. It hit serenity, from a scheme that read me wrong. Met halfway, painted me red and left me tainted.

A new spread forced me to press a stagnant affair and bring it to its knees. It had me hitting the notion, I was taught to release that beast that forced me off the edge, straight into a ditch. I had to repent at every feast where I was given a momentum to break that sanctum.

Warned of what was to come from that outcome, left

torn in every direction. It caused an effect led me to believe I hit a defect, so when I reached my pinnacle the only thing that had me return for another win was the conspiracy that served me well from within.

I had to reclaim what I assumed was the end of that commune. In fact, it was part of a given, that kept growing. They were breeding others to play the same game, just to catch up and feed off the corrupt. It had me on the edge about to gamble what I thought was the last resort.

A second chance, to redeem a theme in between, was a given. Where in the end of that dilemma will hand me a trial and an error. No second to spare, a trend that caused an effect, faced me with a defect. A repeat to a journey that had me defeated. Awarding me with a task that had me on the edge.

I was begging to claim another vision to the game. Where I found myself hitting the end of that domain. Where every trace gave me a rhythm it served me well and handed me a redemption to that mission. It forced me off the edge straight into a ditch that had me regain conscious awareness again.

I was on the mission hitting a competition, it served me a purpose and landed me a role where every thought that come my way was sacred. It served its purpose and had me fast forward to the next level. It handed me the emotional blackmail that had me to press replay all the way.

Where the only task that took its toll had me face another wrath. I had forced my way in; it had me on the edge trapped in the middle and stage a win to that scheme. I had to state a fact, face a trace create a test and repent at every terrible trend. So, when I am about to repeat I hit a dead beat.

The challenge that had me delete, caused an effect and gave me a second chance to praise the lord. I had to face the corrupt and hit back with a trace handing them a failed track record. A challenge that hit a home run forcing the corrupt to return for another given damn taste to that trace.

Serve well at the end of the race. As I returned to fed off the drive that had given me a chance to survive. I had to get back on track press delete, forced to hit back and claim, another beat. So, when I reached the end, the energy will remain the same, creating an anomaly to that trivial pursuit.

It had me face an enactment from a past manifestation. A trend that had me chasing a dream. It ended in a trial an error and final dilemma. Once again, hit a warning a scheme that served me a challenge. It took me on a journey that failed me in between. It had nothing to do with my talent.

It was based on my survival techniquc. There were no freedom and the only thing that had me facing another warning was the last thing that had me withstanding. For that truth pushed me off the edge straight into a ditch no trust just a final faith that served me a rude awakening.

The was no equilibrium a dramatic effect that handed me a theme to the scheme forced the corrupt to return and attempt to redeem a trial and error in between. A trace that gave me a second chance to hit back in advance deleted the true value of an effect that handed a division to the game.

Warning me every challenge had its faults. Every given momentum, had me face a sanctum. Forced to hit back with remorse, while I envision a new mission. Witnessing it all unfolding, had held me hostage while the story untold, revealed. Feeding of the refuge, fall into a captivation, changing my destination.

Trying my luck to get through hell, felt as if I was in a hostage environment. As I continued, to keep up the program, I had locked it in; a world that had me win. The more I remained in that fear, the less I could sense. It took over my sense of reality, I no longer felt safe. An environment that had me trapped.

I was handed a challenge that made me branded. Condensed from my free will, I could not see the positive side I had no freedom to subside. What I had was a trace that served me well at the end of the race. Because I claimed my truth, the energy served me a challenge; worth accepting.

On the condition the collaboration pays for my services. It forced its way in and hit me with another avenue just to revue my point of view. I was on an adventure to another thrill; to learn a new skill. Forcing the corrupt to undo, stand on own ground feed off their own pathway; leave me the hell alone. For I was tired of keeping on common ground, hitting the corrupt with a final sound. A trace at the end of the case A challenge that will surely get me through. Because I fell picked up where I left off pushed the corrupt off the edge, straight into a ditch a challenge that will keep them off my trace.

What I thought was the beginning of a new venture ended up becoming a challenge, like no other. It gave me a reason to hit back with treason. I was seen to be heard, stepping into the unknown an enigma that had me face injustice. Then sent a message to hit back with a trace having me face a case.

Time to clear the air, where the trauma became no more part of the drama. There was a clause and that patent had no reason to break me and leave me unravelling the truth. I was not going to waste another minute pleasing the corrupt by trying to get the truth. For I thought it was part of my journey.

In fact, the project changed it took me in challenged the method and faced another given case. It was meant to be a part of an urgency that had me on the other end pretending again. Where the turn of events, released a task that went belly-up, hitting bankruptcy. It was way too harsh, it perished.

It was beyond the corrupts control, the method became unprecedented. It was part of a vision that had me compose a deploy. A deception, led towards a journey that lined me up for one more chance to propose an accountable to leave the corrupt guessing in advance.

I was taken by surprise left to release a demon from within just to find peace. I was given a chance to release that beast that had me forced to find peace. I had to disclaim and present the corrupt with a brand-new game. A challenge that had me face another prediction to that manifestation.

I was Advised by him who knew to give in or else I will never win. I gave in, fed off the destruction that served me well from within. The last restoration to that manifestation to recover my trend caused an effect. An energy I needed to defect from what I thought was part of an everlasting proposition.

Handed a loyalty card with a brand-new competition. A condition that had me face another proposal to that foundation that took me in and fed off me from within. The assumption forced me to replace, resume and disclaim what I thought will change the commune.

A challenge that met me halfway, caused an effect and allowed me to return. It had me feed off the tremor, press replay at every final hour. It was part of an endeavour, freeing me from that vendetta. A chance to return, feed off the corrupt in advance, holding on to a trace handing me a trance.

The growth to hand the corrupt an avalanche of information; caused an effect. So, when I hit the last resort the energy that served me handed me a second trial; putting me through denial. The mission brought me back to reality. It was part of a journey, that had me on the wrong path.

I was to create a journey that will last. Handing me a constant reminder, I hit rock bottom. The knock on the door, made see how devoted the corrupt were to break my spirit. Clearly, I was on the edge of returning for another pledge. For those who knew had me open to discussion.

It led me towards a path of a whole lot of repercussion.

It had no meaning to me, for the trace was unbreakable and the trend impractical. So, when I reached my peak, the trace will serve me well. It presented me with at face value, an overview to review a clue. Giving me the indication, the impression I was handed had me on the edge reaping another reward.

Ready to impose and feed off the trauma that had me face another case. I was led to believe that the challenges had me focused, it was unravelling an entrance to the unknown. It had me ending that drama that was pending, giving me the impression the trace was part of an intervention.

It was to help me remove the old go back in time repeat the new. All while I was given a chance to return for another review. It had me face a trace, a challenge that was trending. It held me up and handed me a key that interfered with what I thought was part of the attack.

In fact, it was a given to push the corrupt off track. It had me face a personal vendetta that lined me up for a second coming. A challenge that had me forthcoming; an indication I hit a revelation. Where every task took me on a path that had me face a warning; an assessment that had me turned.

I was ready to hit back with a case that will honour me. It handed me an outpour of energy, leading me to a destination where every foundation caused an effect. It handed me the concept to outbreak and carry on to the next outtake. While I outdo the system, get back on track and feed off the mission.

It had me on the edge hounding the corrupt just so I can pledge. For every key that served me well then caved in on the concept and broke the spell now. I was taught a lesson, left forced to hit back with admiration. The key that served me well then handed me the interrogation to settle.

Feeding off the corrupts with admiration, had me hit that upcoming spell. Hounded by the trace that had me a face another given. It had me building walls at the end of the race, so when I reached my peak the corrupt could not return and press delay or delete, for resetting all was not part of that fall.

An entrance to break the system, had me face another mission. For the cycle at the end of that trend had me forced to pretend and hit a hold up. An entrance to that cycle was cancelled and I was on the other end trapped once again. Without fail taught a valuable lesson task that confined the mission.

Repeat after the fact, made me step forward, back on

track. It had become part of a challenge to help me look ahead. It was all out of line, left me to define and have me hit with a severity in mind. Pushing the corrupt off that equilibrium. A task that cut the lead, had no boundary to that service.

A courageous overview took that challenge and had me righteous. It thoroughly forced me to hit back with a survival technique; to push the corrupt off track. All while I was given a chance to free my soul and feed off the corrupt in advance. For what I thought was the last resort had me stating a fact.

A given reason to hit back with treason, a case that had me forced to hit back with remorse. Where the journey I chose was a test that had me forced to digress as I regress. Because I was handed a terrible lie to get by. It had me hitting an indication that the trace had failed.

The warning had sailed, where every manifestation caused an effect. It brought me forward, towards a journey that served me a derivative follow up, towards the other side. I had a breakthrough; I could give in and break the system from within. No longer on edge, wrapped up in a web of lies.

I was waiting patiently for the corrupt to return and hit me with adversity. It took me back in time with a past hurdle that led me towards immortality. A pending trend added a challenge that made me see the only trace that served me well had me conquering a dead end; forced off that spell, into hell.

It served me well in the end, it had me face a dead end. I was given a challenge to restore my energy and reclaim what I thought will help me along the way. In fact, I was back on track, releasing a demon that had me facing an ending that was pending and a trace that left me amused.

I was guessing wrong, forced to hit a hold up, because I was outnumbered. For those who were known to repeat, caused an effect and attempted to alarm me, while they were outfoxing me. They reclaimed their truth by stalking me and I remained on my own. Trying to fake it, so I don't lose another fuse.

I was taken by surprise left to hit back while I supported myself praising the corrupt no longer. It took me in and faced me with a trace and a tremor from within. The phase to that trend used me to rebuild a new feast that forced me to embrace a given piece. For the initiation was left to the imagination.

It had me face another prediction an invasion to the corrupts deception. A decision not taken lightly, nor did it give me the impression I was about to lose a lead to that forthcoming breed. It had me extremely forced to hit back with remorse all while the corrupt were torn terrorising those who warn.

I was on the brink of breaking the system and feeding off the mission that led me towards the wrong proposition. It that had me in military fighting; combat style to the corrupt final arrival. It had me restored by feeding of the trace that had me face another case.

An energy at the end of that trend remained colourful. I stayed in my comfort zone resourceful no longer remorseful. It had changed my train of thought, presenting the corrupt with a chance to remain strong. I had to roleplay every single damn day it was as I was the lead actress in my own movie.

Forced to hit back and break the cycle to a given. A challenge release that bad omen to he who took me misinformed me and led me astray; so, he can win every inning. It had me on the run a trace no mission to replace. A chain reaction that was too hard to break for the cycle had no reminder.

The remainder to it all changed indefinitely and the perception to that redemption, cleared. Handing me the end result I needed to release that beast that forced me off the trace. It was creating a delay to my mission all the way. It was part of a worthy valid response, to that trip that tricked me.

So, when the game became invalid, the journey forced me to repeat. Hitting back with delete. For if the corrupt had their way their would-be hell to pay. I had to face and feed off the trace and lead the corrupt towards a journey that felt wrong all along. But the destination was too hard to bear.

I had to erase everything I was led to believe, wasted another decade trying to succeed. All because the journey was not as long as I hoped in the end, I hit a dead-end. It was based on an intervention that will hand me an enigma to that stigma. For the road to recovery had me fading no longer striving.

I was facing a burnout; handing me the impression I hit the end of that mission. Forcing me to return for one more admiration to that manifestation. No longer was I going to waste another minute, feeding off the trace. It served me the willingness to hit back with stealth, at the end of that wealth.

CHAPTER 7

◆ ◆ ◆

A Chronic Disease The Corrupts Final Cease

I was beginning to think everything was going as planned. Then all of a sudden, my world collapsed. Here I was again creating a challenge that had me refined for a trace that had me face another case. Reformed ready to repeat and stay aligned had the corrupts finally on trial, I no longer living in denial.

A trend that had me face another trace, had me forced to release and prepare for a new key. It had me forced to condition the mission prepare me for a new revision, to that composition. It led me to release and return to compete compel and face another upcoming spell.

So, when I hit that launch it was starting to look as if the early bird had caught the worm. I had to follow up on a trace, stir the pot create a feast so when I caught up, I could redo repeat and press delete. All while I give in and feed off the trauma that served me a willingness to win.

I was taught a lesson led to believe a lie, it served a willingness to give in and get by. The corrupt were stalling hitting with thunder, claiming a trace to repeat and replace another blunder. I was taught a lesson lived a lie created a piece and even forced to release. Stirred the pot then took the initiative.

It had me restored challenged with a key for what I thought was the last resort, gave me a chance to break the system and follow up on another mission. It had me clearing the deck challenge the truth and hit me when I hit the end of that trend that served me the willingness to pretend.

I was on the edge, restoring my energy and reclaiming another debt. I had to repair force my way in hit the corrupt with a dead end at the end of that trend. It warned me that the energy that was surrounded by that key created a greedy outlook that served me willingness to release the beast.

For the energy that had me face trilogy, cause an effect. It gave me a second chance to present the corrupt with a dead end in the end. I hit another overview, trying my hardest to repeat reclaim and face another dead end at the end of that trend. I found myself in the middle of a pickle starting again.

I was hit with a trace, served a sentence to prepare me for a case. I hit the end of that trend, a mission that had me stirred, ready to start again. I was, hitting the wrong intention. Claiming a redemption. Pushing me towards the wrong pathway. Where I had to break the system and create a redemption.

Preventing that traitor, from returning for a yearning. They caused an effect and had me pitch in feeding off the concept so I can get in. I had claimed a division from within. I was to laugh at the entrance test the corrupt at every contest. Face them so I can feed off the concept to hand me revision.

For that preventative angle had me face another trace at the end of the race. For the one thing that had me withstand another informative event, took over the mission and presented me with a brand-new competition. Where the end of that trend, I will be served a revision to help me convert.

Stand my ground and fast forward to the next siren, hinting to me I had no freedom or time to release that beast. It forced me off the edge straight into division that broke me when I fed off the mission. Because I was hit with a vengeance the corrupt were preventing me from holding the key.

It had me face another trace, dividing and conquering a challenge that served me. It had me face another mission, just to release that competition. I had to keep up with the program and prevent the corrupt from returning for a yearning. Everything that came my way had me fight off a bad day.

The warnings were impeccable it had me follow up on a truce entrap he who was on the road to recovery. The trace was part of a given. It had me forced to hit back with trend that broke the system and had me face a dead end. The trial had me hanging from an error to that tremor.

Stirring them at the end of that final trend, caused an effect and presented me with a debt. I had to face another trace, sweeten the deal and feed off the tremor that handed me a delayed reaction to that manifestation. I was taken out of my comfort zone into a trip down memory lane.

The injustice was part of an impurity, given to me where I was trapped in a world that had me face a trace. It was part of a deliverance. Not only I was given reason to hit back with treason, but I learnt a valuable lesson and that the system has one method and the trace has another.

A was given reason to repeat, follow up on a treat, trap those who delete delay and follow upon another bad day. It created a piece, had me forced to hit back and press delete. Then when the troubles subsided, I got to see it all unfold, handing me the trace that served me well.

In the end it was all part of a game that gave me a trend that served me well in the end. I was given a chance to hit the corrupt in advance, where the trace that had me forced to hit back with remorse. Where I get in finalise that win and prepare the corrupt from returning for a yearning.

I was left to interrogate and take a challenge that had me foresee another theme in-between. I had to delay and fail the corrupt all the way. It had me forced to hit back with remorse. Handing me the entertainment that served me a vision. A trace towards a case that returned for a competition.

For the personal vendetta had returned, handing me the invasion that served me a contamination. A task that hinted to me I had no energy to remain holy. Just a version of myself that took me in and prepared me for one more hint a challenge that had me remain heaving at every game.

A version of myself was given, a trend that was forbidden had me facing the enigma to that stigma. The only thing that had me face a task promoted me. It had me condition that mission stepping in the wrong admiration. Handed a clue, a presentation that will skip the corrupts method right through.

I was taught a lesson a long-term effect, a damn trend that hit me with a dead end. For he who was harming, me had me stepping into the truth a challenge that served me well when I hit the end of that spell. For the drama that unfolded was troubling me, had me hit me hit with a warning.

An ending to that saga, I was near the end a beginning

of a trace that had me facing a fear. For the corrupt had me forced to hit back with remorse. All so I can stop them in their tracks and harm them in between. Find a given, an allowance that will hand me the stigma, to reach my enigma.

A chance to return and redeem faced me at every scheme. It had me step into a dead end where the corrupt had me forced to project and follow up on another trace, a given chance to replace the old start new and prepare the corrupt for a dead in the end of that trend.

It had them to release a trend that was pending. An ending that hit me and served me a force that will bring the corrupt forward. It was part of trial and error that will save me from that tremor. I had to find way in and prepare myself for another chance to win. It served me well at the end of that trend.

It gave me a force that hit me back with remorse, so when I reach the trace, I could replace another case. Preventing the corrupt from creating a trend that had me hit a dead end. It served me well and presented me with an ongoing spell. It was troubling me with an outcome that created a dead end.

A feast that had me on the edge, ready to find peace. I had to claim and follow up on another game. Face a trace so when I hit the end of the race, I could undo and follow up on another review. Given the impression the proof they had was golden and I was sitting in the middle about to hit a dead end.

I would of changed and left the corrupt hitting a challenge that had me step into a trace that forced me to release that beast warning me I had no foundation to release what I had was a given a chance to return and hit back with a foundation that will state the fact and follow up on another trace.

I had to get back on track, change what I knew, where in the end I repeat the outcome and report them towards a challenge that served me well. It presented me with a challenge that had me face another trace. A truce that took over, following me towards a journey; that had me face another trial.

I would have stalled long enough to see the journey challenge me. I was back on track skipping the corrupt and courageously hitting back with a curse I could rehearse. Not only I was left for dead, but I had to pick up where I left off. I had to cave in on the concept and release that beast.

I was served well, a habitual ending that handed me peace. The only thing that changed was the last thing that had me focused. I had to rearrange every thought that come my way then when the time come press replay. All while follow up on a brand-new faith that had me release that beast.

It faced me with a test that had me feed off the trauma. It that had me finalise that energy that served me well from. For I had to face was another trauma where he who made me their victim served me the energy that me accomplish goals and follow up on another trace at the end of the race.

Consider the fact and comply with the corrupts method. All so I can get by and then trap the one that had me warned of the outcome. It was the beginning of a new inning. A thought that took me in and presented with an entrance that had me heaving with a vengeance.

I replayed it all in the back of my mind, it had me lead the pact, stay in line and repeat after the fact. The trace became fierce the trend had me on the edge. It took me on a pathway where the trace had no meaning and the energy that forced me to repeat; served me well, it let me go so I can press delete.

Where in the long run it had me face another outcome. It created an expense, so I can catch up and face another thread. Giving me the impression, I had no foundation that will serve me a prize. What I had was the end of that presentation; that had me protest, a given momentum.

It forced me to repeat a sanctum a memory that had me face a trace repeating and old wound so I can clam up and feed off the corrupt. What a reminder had to embrace just to give in and face a warning. The trip down memory lane was too hard to obtain the presentation was a reminder I hit a decipher.

In the end the only thing that had me face another inning was the reality that had me warned the challenge took me in and broke me within. I was taught a lesson left to entrap another given, just so I can catch up and present the corrupt with a final decision. It had me forced to hit back with remorse.

What an ending I had to embrace just to catch up and feed off the race. The given thought that was put in my head, trapped me so I never look or get ahead. The corrupt had me stepping into a harsh reality instead. It was not only a challenge to restore my truth, but it was a given to face my mission.

It was part of a task to see what I had to do to embrace that challenge. The corrupt saw me as an easy target, a final review to face another trace that served me well right through. I had to skip that case that took me in and took over my wing. A reminder I fell into a trap that had me forced to hit back.

But it forced me to hit back troubling the corrupt to get back on track. They were sticking their nose in my affairs but handled me with care they took the initiative and forced me to hit back. Waiting for me to fail so they can prevail. My harsh reality lined me up for a chance to hit back and face a trace.

An ending of the race handing me the inclusion, a trend to that delusion. It was not as representable as I assumed. I found myself challenging the corrupt and hitting a final commune. In the end of that test, it had me force the corrupt to confess a vision that had me foreclose another contest.

It was part of a given a task that hit me with a trial and an error and a final vendetta. It gave me a chance to hit back and face an entrance that served me well; hitting me with a vengeance, as if the trace had me haunted at the end of the race. Taught a lesson and left to reminisce.

Forced my way through and entered the Abyss. It had me on the edge forced to hit back, break the system that left me stranded torn at ever section. Warning me the only thing that had me face an inning was the drama and the lead to make me to believe I was not wrong.

I was pointing the finger at he who had animosity towards me. Time to let go, trick them into an oblivion so I can find my peace. Push them in the corner and create a deception that will fail there every move at every redemption. A path that will serve me a willingness to release the beast.

Meanwhile process every task torment me at every fuss. So, when I reach my pinnacle the only thing that took me in was the drama that trapped me and left me to repeat another win. There was nowhere to turn. I was nowhere near the competition. Just a prize moment that will cause an effect.

It had feed off the trace that handed me a challenge that forced me to hit back with a warning. So, when I reach my pinnacle, I could trust my instincts and start again. Return for a motive and face a new beginning. Trying to fix everything broke me to pieces I could not find peace.

Every drama became a new lease; it took me in and fed off me from within. I was taught a lesson, left to rely on the corrupt to get by. It had me believe every thorough momentum took me in and forced me to face another trial-and-error, preparing me for a final vendetta.

It all unfolded everything, that was not to progress. The whole process had me facing another vision where my mission hit a trial. The drama the tracc the given reason to hit back with treason. The method that took its toll, that had me stepping into a warning a breath of fire to that tremor.

I was to unfold the old the new and the entrance to a pathway I never knew. I was taught a lesson left to repeat, give the corrupt a chance to press delete. Meanwhile delay every communion, that handed me the dysfunction to that union. For gone were the days that had me face another case.

My presentation had me face another reunion, torn at every direction. Whatever I did from this day onwards my name had been already tarnished. It did not make a difference there were several on my raider creeping up on me waiting for me to fail so I never prevail and return for another yearning.

The dream took its toll; I had no time to erase that case. Nor did I have the time invade in the privacy of those who embrace. It was starting to look sinister though; there were creeps everywhere even though who were part of the system were using methods to twist my words around.

I made mark, and regardless of the trace I had no freedom to erase. For the mistake was part of a trap that took me in and fed off me from within. I did not fall for the lie nor the cheating what I fell for was a drama that trapped me and created a brand-new beginning.

The choice was for me to rejoice, and the trend served well in the end. It gave me a second chance to embrace and give in to the corrupt a challenge that became broader that the outcome. A feast that had me forced to hit back with remorse. All because there was no other way out.

I was locked in waiting for the corrupt to own up and face me from within. I realised too little to late the drama was forced to encourage me to enforce and release that beast. It had me face another feast. Where the corrupt were taught a lesson and instead of owning it they were covering up.

The judgements become inevitable the journey surreal. The trace served me well at the end of the race. The assumption embarrassed those who took me in where every trace led me towards a journey that pushed me off the edge hammering me in the head, so I never look ahead.

I had no foundation to investigate nor interrogate and feed off the mission. All so I can invade in the corrupts competition. I had enough I gave in on the condition I win, and they lose everything. With what I assumed, every journey thoroughly took me in and fed off me from within.

I made it to the end I could not return to portray nor pretend. It gave me a second chance to rephrase refill and follow up on another skill. Everything that was to repeat had me face another feat. Every trace had me face an ongoing catastrophe. Where everything that was to go wrong went wrong.

I had to let go surrender and feed off the no show. I had concluded the worse where the energy that had me face a warning and the only way through caused an effect and had me face another defect. For the last thing that had me face a new inning, created a warning that served me, God willing.

I could not breathe; I had no fellowship to succeed. I was handed a repercussion, to that resurrection. Used abused, left to suffer in that perception. I had to release that beast that forced me off the edge, it handed me an evaluation so I can pledge. The drama that served me a reward, for my hard efforts.

CHAPTER 8

◆ ◆ ◆

Just Wait Time Will Tell

The problem was not solved; I could sense the corrupt returning for a yearning. They threw salt to the flame, and the only way I could sense my reality had me facing another gamble to the game. It had me on the edge returning for a yearning. I was taught a lesson left to remain vigilant to that game.

It had me on the edge, trapped in the middle of a trace that had me face another given. The truth had me forced to hit back with remorse, coming to an end was a task that had me break the silence and hit a dead end. It was to clean, then claim all while I remain silent at the end of the game.

It was a given response that had me face another trace. I was forced towards a cause and give in just to claim another win. It was giving me a constant reminder the lie was nothing but truth to get by. A constant repertoire of thoughts that was interfering with my stigma had me return for an enigma.

It had me face a dead end, serving me well and presenting me with an ongoing case. The one thing that had me forced to regain a new improved challenge. A faith that had me forced to hit back with remorse. It was part of a given a momentum a service well and presented with an ongoing spell.

It will force me to hit back and follow up on a rhythmic affair. The one I needed to break the trace and face a given. All so I can return for one more mission. It was part of a process; to lead me to admission but in the end, I was back fighting for my life; firing. Waiting for the corrupt to face another case.

I had to return and fight my way through, progress and press replay. The desired effect had me play the victim that is when I knew I fell into a trap that had me on the edge ready to repeat and replay another gamble to regain a force that took me in and presented with a new beginning.

For what I had seen was yet to be acclaimed, it had me face another trace, ready and willing to look back. The fake the false and the misleading, had me hit a test to revise another conquest. So, when I hit the second trail the method will withstand and face the corrupt with a challenge to repeat a trap.

In the end of that trend, it had me forced to rise above and beyond that dead end. Before they were to return and feed off me periodically. It will take me in and withstand another challenge, all so I can get in and win another informal event. A presentation that will have me cause an effect.

I had to break the silence and repeat that trend. It had me withstand another revision to that mission in the end. I was served a well adjourned case. It had me a consciously aware presenting me with an evaluation to return for another confirmation. For what was to come from that outcome was uncanny.

I had been torn, seen to be believed, sweetened by the thought and betrayed by the scene. The deal had left me reaching my pinnacle. It caused an effect and had me reaping a reward, reaching the edge of reason. Balancing on one leg for no reason because he who knew saw me as a frequent feast.

A trace that had me replaced and repugnant to a trend that had me face a dead end. It had me on the edge ready to please those who perceive and serve me a trend that had me hit a dead end. If it had been left to the imagination before I hit a final evaluation; to cleanse and claim another manifestation.

I was left to live that lie, embrace that trace betray that trend that had me forced to return and start again. I had disloyalty become a constant awareness the energy that stirred the pot. It created a piece that had me forced to hit back with remorse. Trying my luck to uninvite those who were crashing in.

There was no invitation, the interrogation was based on a mission that will hand me a composition that will restore my energy and replace it at every proposal. There was a feast that had me face another key to alarm he who faced me with an external remedy.

They were invading my privacy, more than ever. The trace became a systematic evaluation, that had me face damnation. I was in and creating a trace that will serve me well and present me with a curse that will surely help me come forth. I had to face a trend feeding off the in difference in the end.

It was to claim what I thought was part of the last resort. It was a given, to release that beast that faced me while I caught up and took the energy that served a well attuned sacrament. It had me fade in the middle of that piece. For the corrupt, had me stir the pot, heave at me all while I create a trace.

It had me return and turn a new chapter to that phase. Where we hit the end of the race, I had to face and help the corrupt interface. It had me see the truth and create a challenge that will release the beast. I was sent a package left it to chance so when I looked within that enchanted circle.

The moment past it faced me with a trend. It had taught me a valuable lesson in the end. I had to face a trace, give in to that preach, then when the time come release the beast. For it had me forced to hit back with remorse. I had no choice because the corrupt were on my raider facing me with fear.

It was as if they were in a submarine, advancing their knowledge under the sea. Their vision of civilisation was based on sharks, and other living creatures, that had to survive in that ocean just to remain alive. A vision that had me repeat restore and remind myself that my creativity was fed.

Where sea food is the food for thought and the soul. Red meat was to feed that demon that fed off me whole. Nature wholistically had Harvest those crops, it caused an effect and had me state a fact and create a discernment at the end of that trend that forced me to pretend.

It feeds the natural part of your spirit to help you solve serve and succeed. For every plant you harvest needs to be nurtured in nature to break the natural cycle of Humanity. That is when I knew what I was planting in my body nurtured my natural instincts. The energy I knew kicked in; I on the edge.

I was terribly wrong all along; I thought no one truly cared unless they were handed a chance to return and repair; for what they thought was truth or dare. There was no reality to that scheme that hit me and ran and forced me to hit back in between. It had me restoring my energy forced me to pledge.

They were right in the middle of a trivial pursuit. Where the integrity that served me well ended up forcing me through hell. Every testimonial, had me hit a trial an error and final dilemma. For that trend had me repeat foreclose and start again. A delay that handed me the foreclosure to press replay.

For that trend was the barrier for me to repeat repel and start again. I was taught a lesson, led to believe a lie, I was taken for a fool forced to hit back with remorse. So, when I reached my pinnacle, the journey will be solved and the trace evolved. For the energy created the wrong stirred the pot.

I was reinstated creating an atmosphere that had me stepping inti the unknown. I was taught a lesson and left it to chance creating a defence that had me fight in advance. For the vision was part of a past invasion handing me the incantation to hit back with a manifestation and release to that beast.

For that method had me claim a reservation, to the game. A given momentum that will serve me the train of thought that had me face a given. A reason to replace that case that had me forced to hit back with remorse. I had to hit back with a force, then undo that ongoing review handing me a clue.

So, when the time come hit the corrupt with a failed outcome. The trace that had me face another given gave me a free ride to release and follow up on another piece. It took me in and broke me from within. It will fail the corrupt at every given mission. I had to declare decline and break the vision.

I was given the reason to hit back and face another proposition. I hit the domain; it had me repeating another game. Rewarded by the one thing that had me face another chance to get in. It was part of an unprecedented event that had me step into that debt that gave me a first and last attempt.

I was to hit back and resurrect, just to get glimpse of a future event. I was waiting for the corrupt to remain the same, all while I continue to push them off the edge straight into a case that had me face another trend in the end. Forcing me to redo, reclaim create a journey that had me remain the same.

It had me on the edge restoring my energy and repeating what I thought was the last resort. Convinced of what was to come with an energy that served me well at the end of that spell. It had me thoroughly embrace that trace that left me vague. It was recreating a challenge that had me remain the same.

It had me repeating another stage, frightened beyond repair heaving at every truth and dare. The corrupt had me carrying a trident. It sent me packing before I had a chance to hit back in advance. The true meaning to that drama revolutionised at every cost. Serving me well, while I went through hell.

I had to refer and refrain from informing the truth. It had me curse another verse, refine another trace at the end of the race. I had to inform and reclaim a trace losing another train of thought at the end of the race. it had to compete, claim my game clear my vision and remain solid.

All while I continue to face my fear, clear the air

and then press delete. Giving me the impression I was handed a vision to hit back with a compression. All while I watch the corrupt separate and erupt. I was given a chance without short notice, to create a piece regain conscious awareness and start fresh.

It was on the edge trapped in the middle of a pledge. The trace was trending the trap was never ending on my raider surrendering, trying to get back on track. All because I was let down way too many times. It had come to my conclusion the conviction to that drama was part of a fusion.

No friction and the incursion, it was never based on the contradiction. A theme that never come to fruition. I was chasing a dream that ended up becoming a never-ending conspiracy. The invasion was traumatic. An event where everyone who was involved, wanted to reach out to me and break me.

The challenge was encouraging; the trace was a given. For the mission was permissive and the trend overbearing. It was handing me the evaluation that will stall long enough to create a mission that was interrupting my vision. A defiant method that will leave the corrupt second guessing.

It had me repeating another meeting. All so I never reach my pinnacle, where destitution had me face another resurrection. Trapping me in the end of that resolution. Revolutionising the concept while I trace trap and face another case. It had me hitting the corrupt at the end of the race.

The trace took its toll; I was trying my luck to face my fear overall. It had me forced to hit back with remorse. So, when I reached my pinnacle, I could redo replace feed off the energy that had me face a given. A mission to the corrupts final competition to help me survive, created a journey to stay alive.

I was hitting a hold up, running to catch up. All so I can claim another forthcoming game. They had me face another given, prepare me for a key that served me with a challenge unworthy. Where I had to uncover break the chain and the convince myself I never recuperated from the past.

I remained the same everyone I met were cheating, facing me trying to stop me from succeeding. For what I knew and what it was worth. What was to come from that old outcome, had me remain solid. What it was worth the reminder of the past was not as clear as the vision was part of my admiration.

It took me in and presented me with an upcoming win. For the road I chose was a given it had me face another mission. The results will bring me forward further than ever. For that cycle of events had many dents, Debts and informal Death threats. A drama remained yet to be seen.

For what it was worth, knowing I was hit with a story left to the imagination. The ride to the other side had me winning every destination. It had me foretell a future event that served me a case that had me for close another trace a given reason to hit back with treason.

For what I was sensing it had me remain indigenous to the game. It was absolutely derivative; it served me a chance to hit back in advance unwillingly. For those who knew were conspiring with those who had a clue. Handing me the invalid response, sensing every vision handing me a competition.

It was leading me towards a long-term effect, reviving that debt and handing me a clue. All so I can return and reclaim another overview. I was taught a lesson left to recharge hit a deception and created a journey that served me well. Even though I had no reason to replace that case.

It forced me off the edge straight into hell. It lit a flame restored my energy and pushed me in the corner and drove me insane just to find solace from a game. It had me forced to remain sturdy while the rest hit a home run and forced me to repeat report reclaim and face me at the end of the game.

I saw the light nor grasp for air because the journey I was handed. It was branded and I was in despair trying to claim another division to the game. I was well into the light. It had me face another trace; it was well out of my jurisdiction trying to face another restriction.

For that future event was to put to rest. For that by-stander gave me a chance to protest. I went through hell, took a journey that had me overcome and force me to hit back with a failed outcome. I had to feed off the conclusion with an illusion that wailed while I sailed.

It was part of a conspiracy to disguise the truth. A

challenge that had me refrain frow being rewarded once again. I had to serve my soul, repeat a game that had me forced to remain the same. While I upkeep and trap those who entitled to give in. All while the corrupt scheme to redeem another theme.

Where in the end of that upcoming spell, the drama will evolve. The corrupt will have no choice but to resign and hand me the incursion to that delusion. It served me delusion from that confusion so I can state another inversion to that conclusion, that served me a vision that presentation.

With a goal in mind and a challenge to boot the trace became evil and the measure to that treasure saw me embrace entangle that case give in and break the system from within. Even though the corrupt have no power to revive, upstage and create another challenge at the end of that trend.

There will always be a presentation that will serve the corrupt a final evaluation. I was to hit that ending that served me a deception that had me face another redemption. A challenge that was pending had me forced to hit back. I was given a reason to hit back with treason

A continuation to that saga was, all underwritten. Under a manuscript that had me hit the forbidden with an expense that served me a praise. It forced me to invade evolve and create a substantial amount of energy to stimuli the one thing that had me face another entrapment from within.

It had me face another trial and error and a final vendetta. I had to uncover up another lie and the only way to do so was to take a huge risk and reveal what I was holding on to just to get through. I had to revive remain idling all so I can come alive while the corrupt undertook another raid.

I had to return for undertaking a trend took a turn for the better. For there was no Discretion towards that enigma it created a redemption. No violation to that mission it was a Dirty Lie that Turned into a Dirty Little Secret. It had the corrupt warning me I was nowhere near that proposition.

The trace had me face another trial to that revision. It had revealed the last competition. It showed up at the most awkward moments. So, when I reached my peak the drama and the trace had me forfeit and hand me a trend that served me well in the end.

It was part of a given that served me well at every exposure. It handed me the restitution to cause an effect. A rhythmic amount of energy of fire a failed attempt from heaven to hell. It gave me a second chance to undo and follow up on a review. A test that had me refined, free from the divine.

I knew I hit a second trial and trap to hand me denial. They gave in, saw the path from within and tried to redeem themselves; by twisting my words around. That is when I knew I had to release that beast revive another trace to keep the trend, from repeating again.

Just to regain a new conscious awareness, a vision to claim another competition. A game that served me well, an extreme theme that had me face another vision in-between. For the approach to that creative scene had me face another informal theme in-between.

It was handing me an evaluation, so I hit the end of that reservation. It was causing an effect and claiming another mission at the end of that proposal. It had me face another erosion to that manifestation. Where every given thought, had me remarkably on the edge; strapped in the head.

CHAPTER 9

◆ ◆ ◆

Zenith In Rhodes

I had a spy, who took me in a retreated me from within. It had me create a challenge to help me finalise the energy that served me a final response. The method had become a trial that had me second guessing. Served me a task that started a fight. For that energy that haunted me was a lie.

In the end of that trend, it gave me a presentation to start again. I was left to pretend forced to return, a given reason to reveal the truth. All so I can claim and regain conscious awareness again. For he who had me on his, raider was waiting for me to fail so he can prevail.

For what he did to get to where he was, was a choice. It was made by him who had no reason to harm me in spirit. For his light was dim his trace was a drama from within. It had me step into a lie that served me well, so I never lose nor create a challenge that had me break a fuse.

It caused and effect and created threat; it trapped me in the middle of that sin, so I never see light nor even break that step that had me face another threat. That debt, had me forced to reclaim recall and start again. It stirred the pot essential to that sentiment that had me under investigation.

The evaluation that deserved my peace, had me face another feast. For the right to hit back and face the end of that debt pushed me in the corner and presented me with a curse. It had me refer refine and follow up on an incur. It had made me see the error of those waves a tour to convey a verse.

It hit me with a trade, that served me a validation at the end of that destination. It caused an effect trapped me in the middle of a trace, to help me replace a case. It had me forced to hit back with a final score. Just to repeat tally up presenting me with a conspiracy that contaminated me spiritually.

I was way past that trend that took me in and repeated that win. There was a trace that created a piece forcing me to release that beast. It had me on the edge ready and willing to pledge. More ways than I could imagine, I had to succumb another outcome. A conclusion that handed me fusion.

It had come to be and prepare me for a trend, at the end of that bend. Warning me once again the trace and the treasure was too hard to bear. I had to freshen up then follow up on that dead end that had me scared. I was taught a lesson left to repeat, a given a trace to return for a feat.

In case I was on the other end stopping it from getting worse. As if I was the one to fix the curse. I gave in, just before I was heading for another win. I could not care-less the troubles that come my way was nowhere near the trend that had me face another dead end.

Several were working in unison, under the raider. It was an entertaining notion, part of that trait that handed me a common devotion. The trend was valid; the trace was internal a keynote that led to believe there was no feast. A burden to the beast. A Nonsense, response towards revivification.

A challenge that had me step forward, no reminder to that lead. All it did was break the chain and hint to me I was taught a lesson and left returning for another yearning. All because I fell into a trace that trapped in the middle of a trend beginning for a final delay in the end of that trend.

It had me fast forward facing another trend, at the end; of that final internal bliss. I was given a reason to hit back with treason. A faith less likely for me to release and a presentation that had me hit back and find peace. It had me face a case it led me to believe the drama was too hard to replace.

It forced me to revive a trend, where I had to follow up on a new winning streak. I had to create a piece and break the anomaly that had me repeat. Follow up on the other side of that bend. A key where every journey had me forced to repeat and forge a test just to catch up and progress.

I had to delete then, trouble the corrupt as I burst a bubble. All while I twist their words around to get through. For everything I did and for every journey that had me face another win, had me preach and break the system from within. Where the only thing that served me well was a waste.

It not only had me chasing a dream, but it had also me completing the cause of action. Creating the piece and fast-forwarding towards the next abreaction. So, when I reached the end of that trend the only thing that come to be, was the last thing that had me served a sacred key.

The one thing that will create an anomaly, was the last thing that had me face a trial an error and a final vendetta. A challenge that had me face an inning, a commemorative event forced to undo and vent. Creating a force that turned against me and brought me a new improved journey.

It forced me to redo; repeat replace and follow up on another haste. I was haunted by the past living in the present, laughing at the accusation, hinting to me the journey was too hard to release. A feast that was too hard to undo and find peace a drama that served me good cause.

All so I can catch up and face another trace. It had me undo a review, all while I follow up on another clue. So, when I hit the end of that trend, the only thing that had me face a win was create a failed journey from within. There was a trace that had me repeat report and follow up on a vision.

A trend that stirred me well and had me face another given. They were to return at any given place, where that personal vendetta became part of the haste. I was hit with a finally, left to finalise the outcome to what I thought was the last resort. For the lie had become part of the truth.

A final frontier that had me forced to hit back with remorse. All by lining me up to catch up and feed off the corrupt and I was on the other end trapped in the middle of a dirty little secret. A challenge that had opened the door and once again I'm the perpetrator not the victim.

A victim of scrutiny, haste, rushing it all to catch them in the act of harming me. Made a victim to a conspiracy, that had me stuck once again, on a hate campaign. Where in the heat of the moment start that engine, create war in my peace just to give the corrupt action and justice of the peace.

The method took its toll; the drama had me served with a brand-new role. This time around I was in control, I had it all under control. Even when the corrupt had ignored my plea I still gave in, I still carried my weight. I left it to chance and come out the other end, feeling neglected again.

I'm back to that hate campaign; I hate the world we live in. Those who get in, have the freedom to conspire with whomever; always win. I am always in the back burner suffering in silence trying to make sense why others use me for their own success. My return has now become my; Amen.

I don't wish to hand or bless success, to those who use me stop my, progress. I am constantly handed nothing but drama so they don't confess. The more I offer the more I lose and the less I find that my progress has any sort of success. Because I hate those who use me for their own growth.

For they assume I am here for them for the long haul. In fact, what I offer is no decipher to that drama that they see when I say no to their reality. It is my way of accepting a backlash of those hideous events that had me face another conquest. In fact, I fell for the tact not the trace.

It gave me permission to repeat repair, replace find out where it all begun. Face another incur that had me stir the pot challenging in the end of that trend occurred and create a trend that served me well in the end. So, when I caught up, I could break the chain and save myself from another bad day.

Releasing that demon that had me forced to hit back for no reason. It gave me the permission to repeat and restore my energy at every informative season. I was served well no wisdom nor knowledge just a failed attempt to bring humanity back to reality.

Stating facts and repeating another informality, served me well. It gave me a second chance to repeat every trace in advance. I might as well follow up on a given, a reason to repeat and report the corrupts mission, for no reason. Just to reclaim and catch up on another game.

The follow up was part of a trace that led me to believe I had no freedom nor foundation to follow up on another competition. The fellowship was a lie where the tradition was part of a mission, creating a never-ending response a trace that served me well at every proposition.

All so I never get by for the trend was a given it had me hit the end of that trace. It brought me back to what I thought would become the last resort. The concept had trapped me, those who entered my realm had to invade in my privacy and create a travesty just to challenge me at every diversity.

Assuming my role in their vision is to help them complete their mission. The more they saw the more likely I was to embrace another division to the case. For there was no curse, there was no verse and the only thing that handed me the trial was an error and a manifestation to that tremor.

It was part of a trick of the trade, that served me well at the end of that raid. There was no trend no failed attempt just a reason to accommodate and follow up on another attempt a curse I was to reverse and a key that had me foreclose another trace at the end of the race.

A key to serve me well, presenting the corrupt with an upcoming spell. The curse was way too heavy to evolve. A reason I hit the energy that served me another season. It was because the corrupt forced me to validate and carry on to the next feat a task served well while I repeat a spell.

The trend served me another deity, so when I reached the point of no return. I was given the reason to hit back with treason. A challenge that will repeat and hand me the incantation to return and press delete delay and follow up on another key a test that will serve me a high priority.

It had me facing an interaction that was on the level of satisfaction. It forced me to break that tradition. It led me towards the next proposition, a way of excepting that final division. It took me on a journey that tore me. A proposition, that took me on a mission that had me press replay.

The journey I was on, had me relying on the corrupt once more, to remain strong. I was taught a lesson left to the imagination. Where every personal vendetta gave me a chance to hit back with an allegation. I was put in a position worse than the imagination, waiting for the corrupt to face me.

An investigation that was long overdue, I was led to believe that the energy was too hard to conceive. So, when I hit the overload the corrupt had me stand guard, facing an armour. I was taught a lesson left it to chance so when the corrupt saw me easy the journey was heavy.

I was humble, trapped in the middle of a scheme. A theme that had me face another drama in between. Trim prim and proper, was the way to go and even then, the energy served me well. It took me in and reserved me the right to undo a scheme in between. A trace too hard to replace.

It had me step into an advance threat, a tread that had me forced to release that beast. It gave me an opportunity to face another trial, a trivial pursuit that handed me denial. It caused an effect took me in and broke the system that had me full steam ahead, waiting for the corrupt to erupt.

For what I had to offer, gave me a sense of reality. It had me foretell and appreciate what was to offer; all while I went through hell. For the less I knew the better the review it had me face another overview debating what drama will come and what Karma will overcome the outcome.

Less was to be aligned; and more was to be replenished the less I saw thew more I had to claim for every given moment was given a bad day. For no recognition to claim that competition had me face another mission to that vision. It had me forced to hit back with remorse, that proposed me a clue.

It was handing me the invasion to that incursion, that served mc an evaluation. It stalled long enough for me to wish the corrupt catastrophe, just to screw he who knew and follow up on he who had a clue. It had me shape up the corrupts motivation to that manifestation.

It had me claiming the truth, clarifying what I knew. So, when I reached the end, the only thing standing tall was the drama that had me face an aroma to that sentiment. I was to return and face another trace at the end of the race. Forcing me to redo and disclaim another overview.

I was handed an incantation to enter the realm of an expectation; that did not come to fruition. I was served an alliance at every manifestation. It served me an evaluation that had me question the corrupts final. For he who had me face a mission to that composition became violent.

I had to stall, give in feed off the mission and break the competition. Where the drama became solvent. The method was unravelling my head, had created a trace with no credibility. It took me in and had me face another violation to that credibility that served me a choice from within.

It had me face another cause and effect. It was presenting me with a gift that had me forced to reject. Where the only way I could look ahead was create a journey that had me forced to hit back with remorse. Because every journey, had me mirror a deception, to that redemption.

It caused an effect took me in and faced me with a tremor that failed me from within. There was a drama that took me in it had me face another trial and error and a trauma that forced me to reclaim and grasp for air in the end of the game. For I was left to consider face another wither.

So, when I hit the enigma, the journey that followed served me a key. It was handing me the resolution I needed to repeat repel and follow up on another forthcoming spell. It had me withstand an entitlement trapping me with clear conscious. That is when I knew I was served the wrong clue.

So, when I reached my pinnacle, the trace became a vision; that restored my intuition. Where every pattern had a motive, it handed me redemption that served me a deception. Haunting me at every validation. Warning me the result created a stigma that caused an effect and handing me restitution.

I needed to resurrect, but the concept turned against me. He who knew, had other ideas, putting me down was there way of covering up the truth. Making me out to be a fabricator, a perpetrator and instigator. Victimized by scrutinising me with those values that had me face another sacrament.

Fe he who knew could not wait to team up with those who had a clue. Just to screw me right through. For the thoughts in my head were beginning to look like I saw the light. The trace had me face another case it had me facing another reality that was troubling me it left me to repeat.

All so I never get back on track and feed off the trend that had me face another dead end. A trace that stirred the pot. Where I had to claim, feed off the game, find my way through and give in to an existence that served me a persistence. A restoration that handed me an animation to that enigma.

As if I was not as vigilant, as I meant to be. For I was headed towards a journey that handed me a test. It had me face another trace, giving in as the journey unfolded. I was tormented by the lie trying to get by. It had me trapped in the middle of a line up led to believe that the drama was a tie.

Praised by the trade, left to erase the case. Where the dream became a reality, a given tread that served me well and handed me a given. A reason to belt the corrupt for no reason. It had me erase the case and Forsee a future event, where the corrupt undo another review.

It was enough for me to witness the journey unfold. It was not as lit as the dream permit. It was meant to release, and face me with a piece, where it had me face another feast. For those who had no freedom nor foundation to get ahead. Searched for answers energised by spirits.

For he who sat on my raider took me further. Assuming using me with an intimidation will hand them validation. Where the answers they needed to break me and leave me forced to hit back with remorse. Forged that caused giving me the trend to hit the corrupt back with a dead end.

A method was created in unison to he who found me easy. I had to break my spirit, attempting to hit me at the end of that follow up. It was a fellowship that took me in and reported me towards a journey that had me face my true reality. For the energy that took over, was part of a trend.

It was a product of the corrupts final debt. It hounded me in the end, facing me with a dead end. The tradition of that mission served me a proposal that saw me as an easy target. A trap that had me face another trend in the end. Forcing me to give in and break the emotional blackmail from within.

CHAPTER 10

◆ ◆ ◆

A Stepping Stone Where The Chaos Became Unknown

I had to fight for my life, and obviously in this stage, fighting back was well overdue. Not only I was left with a buck, and a measly dollar in my purse. To my defence my pulse was still beating my stomach full, all needs met. My life was presented with a gift that kept giving.

But envy took me on a journey not worth living. Where every time, I was let down I was set up by the corrupt. They saw me as an easy target, trying my luck to embrace another case. All while I attempt endure a dream that forced me off the edge straight into a dilemma;

served a tremor.

It had me on the edge wedged in the middle of an inquisition. For the corrupt were in competition. I had so many on the other end pretending they cared. Waiting to see where they can fault me, so I fail, hit a dead-end and watch my life crumble. While I fall crawl failing it all, once and for all.

It was leading me to a destination that had me forced to release the beast. The fact they were competing with me had me forced to throw a flare in the air. Putting me through hell all because they could, had me cornered. Wasting a day trying to come to terms with the fact I was too easy.

Ready and willing to hit back with a chilling repertoire. I was taught a lesson and left to repeat a treason. The method was cunning the road forthcoming. The trace was a given, and the dream was part of a space in-between. Where the trend and the interaction pushed me off the bend.

It had me facing a theme where the corrupt could create a journey yet to be seen. A report that led me to gamble my dream away, had me holding on to another bad day. A challenge that took me in and faced me with a trip down memory lane. All so they can get an attempt to win another inning.

I was forced to release that beast I could not get out of that feast. There was no test the progression was part of the interaction and even though I had to undo and follow up on another clue. I had to face my doubts. Accomplish a goal and follow up on a new improved role.

Because the corrupt saw me easy; ready and willing to feed off me. I was trapped in the middle of an extreme event, where every dream had me redeem another scene. I was living in-between the scam the scheme and whatever the corrupt had created while moving with the theme.

It was forcing me to come to terms with old the new and faith that I once I knew. A challenge that had me on the edge facing another pledge. A trace that had me preach, my truth. A stepping stone towards my reality. A strength that had me on the edge, reckless; waiting to break the silence.

It had me feed off the trend that served me well a trace that had me forced to hit back with a case that had me cursed ready to embrace and follow up on a given a method. It had m hit the forbidden a challenge that saw me repeat. A trend that had me forced to repeat and start again.

It had me forced to ease my pain, feeding off the chain reaction. It had me forced to return for an abreaction. With a certain degree of sanity added from the irrationality. It held me hostage, so I never succeed, for the corrupt were given a reason to hit back and feed off the trace.

The treason was the reason, I was torn, hit in the middle of a curse. Just to get a glimpse of a future endeavour. The corrupt stood its ground and forced me to hit back with an expense. It was presenting me with a trace that had me profiting that energy creating false synergy.

Serving me on common ground, from that haunting became exhausting. Forced to release that feast, that had me foreclose an ongoing restoration to that manifestation. So, when I caught up, I could undo and feed off the trauma that failed me and fed off the tremor, serving me a final vendetta.

So, when I landed securely the troubles were branded. It had me release that feast, in the middle of a curse. Where it had me forced to rehearse and trap trace and present the corrupt with a true rude awakening. Where everything that come my way turned me down and had me press replay.

It left me upside-down waiting for me to fail so I never sale. It took me on a journey that had me face another given. A dream that served me a vision to create and counterplay, towards an everlasting proposal. A competition that had relisted handed me results with a journey that served me.

I was way ahead of myself, the path I was on had me head strong. Those who witnessed my strengths, saw me a threat. Took advantage creating a lifelong debt. I was heading towards a journey that had me forced to look back. It caused an effect creating a task to help me pay off a debt.

As if I was the one that created the final outcome. The end of that trend caused an effect; it had me play the game that hurdled putting the corrupts plan to rest, just to remain silent in the game. It had me gamble the one thing that caused an effect. It brought that enemy to his knees, failing with ease.

I was returning once again, back on track, an attempt to break the cycle and state a fact. All while repeating that trend that pushed me in the corner. Leading me to a destination that broke the silence. Creating a brand-new destination was inevitable, it hit the end of that cycle.

I was the one that served the corrupt a challenge, that had me on the edge. I had to release that beast that forced me to return look ahead. I had to break the system that took me on a journey that release that demonic effect. I had to revive reveal and remain earnest to the game.

All because I was shaken up, by that lie, it took me in and fed off me from within. It had me proving the corrupt wrong. Warning me that the edge of reason had me face another treason. It was causing an effect and stabilising that truth. It had me repeat report while I break the cycle.

It created an anomaly; an impression I hit the end of that season. Where the corrupt saw the whole thing come to fruition. I had the freedom to break that trend that was taunting me. It forced me to reveal revive, start fresh again. It was leading them to a destination that had me facing a reservation.

Giving me the impression I was left to lift my spirit on my own. No longer had me waiting for the corrupt to return. I had to face a trace at the end of the race. I wanted to plea, then flea, be heard and not be rejected frequently. My faith in humanity relentlessly stalled and held me hostage.

It took me on a path holding on to the past. It forced me to redo, disclaim and follow up on another game. The journey was old the trace evolved, so when I hit the end; the story was told. It had cleared, cleansed and handed me the enigma to catch up and clear the air and start again.

It was holding on to that old rag, that was saturated with a toxicity an energy that had me step into the unknown. A stinge that reminded me the life I led was nothing but a bad omen in the end. It was part of a given, a chance to hit back with admiration. to that destination that served me a purpose.

I was left to repeat, taught a lesson, while giving in. Where my impression to that journey was not as admirable as I wished. I hit a conflict of interest, with restriction. It handed the corrupt a chance to return and hit me with a key. A given reason to trade in, trap and follow up on a new version of me.

In the end of that keynote, I saw the end of that challenge hit a hold up. For what I thought was the last resort, hit a test that had me foreclose another given. I had to interact then give the corrupt a chance to counteract. So, when I hit the end of that trivial path that test will not last.

Where the only thing that come my way was the last thing that served me a replay. I was served a well-deserved and desired note. Forcing me to return and repeat another key hitting me simultaneously. It was cunning how the troubles forwarded and how the trend served me a trace.

It had me forced to hit back and follow up on a given; a reason to hit back with treason. I was hit in advance and watch it unfold. Handing me the incur to create a force to hit back with remorse. The journey challenged me and handed me a verse to that curse, that took its toll and foreclosed.

I was to return to that theme, that had me scheme in-between. For those who knew became speechless. They wanted me to believe it was my fault and everything that was said and done had to do with the outcome. I was tormented with disbelief disclosing another failed attempt.

It had me on the cleanse, with a task, warning me there was no pressure. It served me a blend that gave me a chance to embrace a trace that pushed me in the corner. It had requested a division to that mission. Warning me the entity to that test, was the trouble that had the corrupt confess.

That game was sitting in my domain, tormenting me. It gave me a second chance to ease my pain. I had to release that demon, that had troubled me. That is when I knew the focus was on me, never getting through. The dream was a task that had me forced to hit back with a curse.

A trial that could not be reversed, nor rehearsed come

from within. For what served me first had come to be, handing me the rehearsal to survive that dive. It was part of a test, that handed sections branded with a sacrament. It leaned towards a final frontier, a point taken after it was given.

The conspiracy erupted and become known. That is when I knew that case was closed the drama unfolded. He who used me to claim his thoughts saw the error of his ways. I fell into a tremor that taught them never to erase nor trace a case. Because the trauma is way too hard to replace.

They would enter my realm and face me with an enigma to that stigma. Handing me the second trial that served me denial. Repeating what I thought was the last resort. To my defence it was the beginning of a brand-new inning. A challenge that will face me when I hit the finally.

I had given the corrupt a chance to come forth, and undo that review. Confess, to that deception, repeat after the fact, before it became fiction. Because it was all done behind my back, it had me facing hell, lined up for a key that served me unwell. I hit a downside and its broken heaven's gate.

Those who chose and were not meant to enter, caved in on it. Entered as if they were welcome in fact I never knew and those who were torn left me suffering in Heaven right through. The ride to the other side was unsettling I could not trust a living soul. Whomever entered had me fragmented.

It forced me off the edge straight into a narrow pathway. Where the one that was left, had me guessing wrong, returned to repeat and follow up on another trace where this time around they try their best to repeat rebel reach out to me and once again attempt to put me through hell.

after I hit a home run had me suffering once again as if he won and I never knew and the outcome to that foundation brought him a brand-new manifestation. For the corrupt were hitting a final round up, and I on the other end wasting no time because I faced another warning.

It had me returning for a yearning claiming my truth; left to the imagination. It was restoring the truth and presenting me with incantation to break the trend that forced me to repeat and repel against the corrupts final damnation. I hit a spell once again, facing what I thought was the end.

For that trend that took me in and fed off me from within had me on the edge, trapped with a debt. Where once again I had one foot in the door and the other inactive. Where it stood clear on the outside trying to release that beast that had me forced to return and find peace.

Pushing and shoving to get in and I on the other end trying to catch up and face another case. It had me cause an effect all while the corrupt line up for another hold up. While I get in and praise that test that served me a challenge to help me rely on the corrupt no longer to get by.

I was left to release face another feast, so when the time come, I could undo and reach my peak. I could look back repeat and press delay, deny, delete, reset that debt as I rise above and reject it all. Deepening my soul so I can rise above that fall that handed me the energy, that served me a wall.

A long-term effect of trinity had come to reality. A trend that had me reliving a dead end. A trace that had me trending, no longer pending, because the corrupt forced me off the trace, straight into a rough spot. It was warning me I hit a dead end. A challenge where I no longer need to pretend.

I fell and forced my way out of hell. The energy that created it all so stated it. A trend to hand me a curse at the end of that verse. For every forthcoming spell, had me face another stealth to that remedy. I was put through hell. Warning me the only thing that stood to win was a waste of space.

I was served well from within all while I watch the corrupt failure and lose that hint of sadness that led them towardness madness. I had one more chance to prove I was innocent for the corrupt were ganging up on me to get my attention. It got to the point they terrorised me just for redemption.

Once more, I was heading for an encore, for what it was worth the drama become a key. It served me a dead end a death threat and final frontier, periodically. The corrupt had to face me with a thorn, leading me towards a journey less likely for me to release; more likely for me to find peace.

The test had me foreclose a challenge; it had me enter the unknown. It gave me a chance to witness in advance the stalking was a test. The energy surrounded by it was reviewed and I was renewed, the only thing that had me face a trace from within was replaced with another given case.

It was part of an inning to create a challenge that was misleading. It had me looking for answers that were silent. It gave me a second chance to look beyond and beware of what will come from that outcome. I was given the freedom to be aware of my surrounding and repeat after the fact

Where the only thing that had me face another inning was the least thing standing. Where I get to witness the ending create a barrier between he who knew and he who had a clue. Even then the troubles were hard to bear, for the corrupt were given a challenge that was invading my privacy.

I hit a final the ending was part of a given, so I catch up and face the corrupt. It was part of a trace that had me forced to hit back with a brand-new case. A given reason to release that beast let go and find peace. Just to catch up, break the cycle and revival, where the corrupt change that recital.

For every challenge was part of a treaty, and I was given a reason to hit back with treason. All because everything that come my way had me face another warning every step of the way. It added a drama that had me forced to hit back and create a challenge that was part of a creative sense.

I was led to believe the lie was part of a drama, that had me forced to hit back with remorse. I was taught a lesson left to embrace another trace at the end of that forthcoming case. It served me well forced me through and gave me an indication I was lined up for an investigation.

A brand-new case that released that beast, had come to fruition. Where the corrupt had no reason to invade in my privacy. Follow up on another treason, entertaining me with the notion that the conspiracy was purely to stir the pot and feed off the trend that took me on a journey to start again.

It had me forced to hit back and face a trial, a given reason to restore my final arrival. An energy to face a formality come to fruition, that is when I knew I hit an incur. Intervening in my affairs while screening was there way of getting their desire to harm me fed.

They took me in and faced me with a traumatic event from within. Where every time I wrote I burnt so the corrupt could re-enter and I lose another fuse. It was handing me a winning streak that served me bad news. All because their plot was to push me off the edge, so I lose the plot.

The energy that was harming me, left me stirring the pot. For I was lined up for a chance to release that beast. A challenge that gave the corrupt a piece of their own feast just to prove to the corrupt I was innocent it was all a misunderstanding a troubled event that had me forced to repeat.

It was part of an inner feast, that had me forced to foreclose an inning to that scene. I was brought forward into an extension that handed me the faith that restored that redemption. A challenge that was open to discussion a trace that served me well at the end of that forthcoming spell.

I was forced to hit back with remorse. A challenge that took me in onto a new review. A final explanation to that manifestation that warned me; I was way off the planet. For anyone who understood was left to delay, under the impression the road I was on was just the beginning.

It was based on a case that served me wrong for way too long. Those who knew were on my raider trying to use me to get through. Every motive had a test, and every foundation took me in and fed off me from within. Troubling me on a daily basis because I would not give in.

The worst was a curse left to the imagination. Where I was storing energy feeding off the synergy that led me towards a journey that had me face my Eulogy. In the end they got their wish my ceiling collapsed the flood come through and the corrupt come running to save me.

As if it was all prewritten by he who wanted to face me and feed off my energy. He saw me as an easy target. Led me towards his direction that had me manifesting a deception to prove my innocence and theory. All it did was make things worse, it gave the corrupt a chance to curse.

I was stuck trying to fight off those who were on my raider, warning me to give in or else there will be hell to pay. It caused an effect and created a piece it had me forced to hit back, just to find peace. The road became disloyal the trace created an enigma; I stuck trying my hardest to undo a review.

I could not fight back, because if I did my words would be twisted and my thoughts revised. Those who were requesting to destroy me were on my raider leaving me hitting a final degree. Warning me the only thing that had me face another inning; was the last thing on my mind.

I had to declare another warning. Scheming once again to follow up on another dead end. It became a prewarning and I was stuck knocking on Heaven's door again. With nothing to show for hard earnings. I was praying for everyone to succeed just so I can get out of this bad omen.

It handed the corrupt a chance to belt me in advance. They created a war in my peace purely to catch up. Just to catch me in the act, follow up on a conspiracy that pushed me off track. for those who yearning to return for another theme to break me in-between handed me huge conundrum.

I gave in, I had no choice their method took over my life. They had me screaming for help and no one come. Only when I gave in and handed the corrupt a chance to blame me for everything. They were on my door knocking and laughing at me once more; just to claim another encore.

They were coming droves, purely to push me off the edge; to stir me up and drive me crazy. All so they can get another crack at a theme that was never meant to be part of the scheme. Their plan was to make me out to be the perpetrator. I was not the enemy I was truly belted with scrutiny.

I had nowhere to turn nothing to say, all I knew the corrupt were hitting me with heresy. I was cornered speechless. The ceiling collapsed the flood took over and here I was again dealing with he who created that piece. Waiting re-enter harming even more asking for war, while I asked for Peace.

The only way out was to give in and pray to God from within. I don't lose my life trying to fight off a trader siting on my raider. I hit the end my head torn, on the edge, breaking the rules and starting fresh. A whole lot of drama come my way I had to look ahead and try my best not to lose my head.

I was a victim to a trace that gave them the power to undo and devour. The task was prewritten and I was stuck hitting a warning. My anxiety kicked in, and whomever I met along the way were shocking me from within. I could not trust a living soul and here I am, once again, God Willing. AMEN

ABOUT THE AUTHOR

Panagiota Makaronis

I am not going to boast about myself, my education my family values or views. In the end what can I say life is what it is and everyone has their presentation.

What level of education I have is not important here, the fact that I have lived through death threats, dead ends, and the Demons in my head is enough for me to say! Good reddens, to hard labour.

Life to me has been nothing but expectations with several disappointments, on the hope I get somewhere trusting people when they were meant to help me was another story.

Having said that how many times have I heard people say I am helping you, I let my guard down and it ends up a never-ending Drama a story. Where if I was to repeat will end up worse than the first.

Every goal I set for myself so far though, I have achieved. This book is one of them.

But at what expense I had to endure, just so I do not lose faith in myself and in Humanity along the way. Others who knew could not wait to trace test my patience on the hope they erase my passion and end the race before me.

Because I was living and breathing in a society full of competitors, trying to compete with me and entering my realm on the hope they can harm me for they assumed that had more man power than me.

My theory is just to prove that the world is Governed, not just by everyone you meet but also by the way you witness and see yourself. It plays a huge part when you are about to end one journey and rehearse a new path.

A journey I wish not to return and replay, if anything I just want to move forward not look back and return for revenge. Because my opponent lost a fight and could not harm me so he decided to alarm everyone on the hope they cave in on it start an Allianz and harm me that way.

It left cursing the ones who were reversing and rehearsing, just so they can return stir the pot and leave me stagnant. Stuck in a world of my own sitting in self-pity, no way out unless I fought my way out.

That created more war in my peace because those who knew me, knew me well, fighting back was the only way they can prevent going through hell.

In the end all it did, was make things worse, for they were making mountains out of mole hills. However, the interpretation was enough for me to see I was on the right track the risks I took was based on not losing my faith or myself because others were doubting me and create anomaly.

They were haunted by me and my spirit they could not handle my presence or wait to see where they could hit me and run with a dead-end challenge. The only way out was to hold on to my dream repeat rebel and hit with an All might Spell.

I had come across several individuals who could not wait to break my fighting spirit, constantly on the move of how to kill me and my spirit.

The constant rejection, let down from those stalkers who had nothing better to do then follow me everywhere. Enter my realm just before I am about to make it happen, it got to the point I was failing every test because of it.

Eventually I gave in it was evident, let my Guard down on the hope and the condition there abuse and their method return and back fires.

Having to pick myself up after being pushed straight of the edge from so called Evil! Family friends and Associates, those who I call the corrupt.

What can I say a job is a job well done, level of education is based on life lessons? Everyone has a theory and so do I. Whether you agree is another story to just agree to disagree.

All the studying I did gave me an outlook, a method and outcome where sometimes I look back and wish I never entered but again I would not be here if I didn't.

The theory of here see and speak no evil to me is a lesson lived and lesson learnt. A challenge I can honestly say, it was testing a trace for me to embrace look back and erase. As I face my fears overcome another failure to that feast that handed me release.

As I look ahead and watch my journey unfold with a story untold, it will become a final phase to the next part of my truth. A challenge that will give me the indication I was on my path a feast to release peace.

Everyone is looking for answers and the hope to live through life with comfort passion and a reason without having to deal with treason.

My memoirs are based on my journey and life lessons, it

is all in the book in the end only time will tell, what can I say will be me, keeping up with the programme my way.

Not the way they state it because I hesitate to wonder who is really saving me here. For in the end the matter of facts, is in my hands, because I am an individual. My thoughts are based on my life lessons and no one can challenge or change that.

I know every challenge has its presentation and what I see is I am about to shut one door and open another. Where my vision is no longer impaired and whatever is enlisted to get to this point is no longer in the back burner.

It belongs in my spirit it is mine I earned it! I am just messenger, just passing through the rest remains Ancient History added with a Mystery.

For those who read will understand read between the lines, because my point of view is a venture to next quest on hope I can make a difference to humanity for the next generation to read and interpret my vision as a composition not a competition!

Happy Reading!

BOOKS BY THIS AUTHOR

The Theatrical Melodia Of My Life : Chronicle One

This book is based on my journey, the roller coaster I call life, my thought patterns, and my experiences. How I overcome so many turmoils, how I changed my perception, for it led me towards a destination that gave me tension. Where I felt I had no freedom or free will; all I had was failure. Added with faith, and the hope to overcome another fall. Feeding off the concept as I rise above it all!

Crucify The Holy Spirit While You Sacrifice A Soul: Chronicle Viii

Crucify the Holy Spirit while you Sacrifice a Soul, Chronicle VIII is the continuation of the Melodia of my life KREA PREA (TM). An Epistemology, My Odyssey call it My Bible I swear by it. The difference is my one speaks in volumes and Chronicles. I speak the truth and in tongue.

Entering The Kingdom Of Oblivion: Chronicle 14

Working towards Entering the Kingdom of Oblivion; Chronicle 14

A method that lined me up for a rude awakening. Where the corrupt tracked me down, restored their energy by summoning me. A key, that was stolen from me was relisted and I was returning to retrieve it. I left it to chance, then let my guard down because I was let down.

Poetic Justice A Pathway To Transition: Chronicle Xix

Poetic Justice A Pathway to Transition Chronicle XIX is the continuation of The Theatrical Melodia of my Life. A Prophecy, preventing me from losing my identity; working towards my passage way of serenity. Where I found myself hitting an interpretation, handing me an investigation

Agrius A Rise Above The Antichrist Chronicle Xxi

Agrius A Rise Above the Antichrist Chronicle XXI is the continuation to Theatrical Melodia of My Life. I was on a pathway, towards a presentation, to lead me to the next destination; only to hit a hold up. An obstacle come my way; a pending trap. I remained repentant, just to get back on track.

Burning Crown Of Glory: Chronicle 25

I found myself in a position of questioning the motives of certain individuals. I was put in a situation, that had me forced to override, run hide, and return when needed. The clock was ticking, and those who were relentless and ruthless were scheming. I could not fight back, I felt I was ganged up on.

The Temple Of Zeal : Chronicle 27

The Temple of Zeal Chronicle 27; is a renewal, to ground me from an old wound. My attention to detail brought redemption. I could sense my reality changing, from recovery into deception. Returning to hit back with passion; burnt out. Releasing the demon; as I pause an effect.

www.ingramcontent.com/pod-product-compliance
Lightning Source LLC
LaVergne TN
LVHW020631100826
845148LV00012B/2137

* 9 7 8 1 7 6 4 4 5 8 1 3 9 *